Resurrection or Resuscitation?

What Really Happened in That Tomb?

By Eileen McCourt

Resurrection or Resuscitation?
What Really Happened in That Tomb?
By Eileen McCourt

CONTENTS

ABOUT THE AUTHOR

Eileen McCourt is a retired school teacher of English and History with a Master's degree in History from University College Dublin.

She is also a Reiki Grand Master teacher and practitioner, having qualified in Ireland, England and Spain, and has introduced many of the newer modalities of Reiki healing energy into Ireland for the first time, from Spain and England. Eileen has qualified in England through the Lynda Bourne School of Enlightenment, and in Spain through the Spanish Federation of Reiki with Alessandra Rossin, Bienstar, Santa Eulalia, Ibiza.

Regular workshops and healing sessions are held in Elysium Wellness, Newry, County Down; New Moon Holistics N.I. Carrickfergus, County Antrim; Spirit 3 Ballinasloe, County Galway; Angel Times Limerick and Sacred Space Newbridge, County Kildare, where Eileen teaches all of the following to both practitioner and teacher levels:

- **Tibetan Usui Reiki levels 1, 2, 3 (Inner Master), 4 (Teacher), and Grand Master**

- **Tera-Mai Reiki Seichem**

- **Okuna Reiki (Atlantean and Lemurian)**

- **Reiki Karuna (Indian)**

- **Rahanni Celestial Healing**

- **Fire Spirit Reiki (Christ Consciousness and Holy Spirit)**

- **Mother Mary Reiki**

- Mary Magdalene Reiki

- Archangels Reiki

- Archangel Ascended Master Reiki

- Violet Flame Reiki

- Lemurian Crystal Reiki

- Golden Eagle Reiki (Native North American Indian)

- Golden Chalice Reiki

- Golden Rainbow Ray Reiki

- Goddesses of Light Reiki

- Unicorn Reiki

- Pegasus Reiki

- Elementals Reiki

- Dragon Reiki

- Dolphin Reiki

- Pyramid of Goddess Isis Reiki

- Magnified Healing of the God Most High of the Universe

- Psychic Surgery

Recent new venues include Celtic School of Sound Healing, Swords, County Dublin and Holistic Harmony, Omagh, County Tyrone.

This is Eileen's **14th** book.

Previous publications include:

- *'Living the Magic'*, published in December 2014

- *'This Great Awakening'*, September 2015

- *'Spirit Calling! Are You Listening?'*, January 2016

- *'Working With Spirit: A World of Healing'*, January 2016

- *'Life's But A Game! Go With The Flow!'*, March 2016

- *'Rainbows, Angels and Unicorns!'*, April 2016

- *'........And That's The Gospel Truth!'*, September 2016

- *'The Almost Immaculate Deception! The Greatest Scam in History?'*, September 2016

- *'Are Ye Not Gods? The true inner meanings of Jesus' teachings and messages'*, March 2017

- *'Jesus Lost and Found'*, July 2017

- *'Behind Every Great Man........ Mary Magdalene Twin Flame of Jesus'*, July 2017

- *'Out of the Mind and Into the Heart: Our Spiritual Journey with Mary Magdalene'*, August 2017

- *'Divinely Designed: The Oneness of the Totality of All That Is'* January 2018

Eileen has also recorded 6 guided meditation CDs with her brother, composer and pianist Pat McCourt:

- *'Celestial Healing'*

- *'Celestial Presence'*

- *'Cleansing, energising and balancing the Chakras'*

- *'Ethereal Spirit'*

- *'Open the Door to Archangel Michael'*

- *'Healing with Archangel Raphael'*

Eileen's first DVD is now available, **'*LIVING THE MAGIC'*,** a live recording, in which Eileen deals with many aspects of spiritual understanding, and challenges many of our long-held beliefs including Mary Magdalene and her relationship with Yeshua, the great awakening now taking place right across all of humanity, the true nature of God, life and death and much, much more. We all need to get the truth before we can proceed or even start on our soul evolutionary path, and Eileen, in this riveting DVD, exposes the truths that we need to know at this time in the history of creation, when the collective consciousness of all humanity is moving rapidly into a higher vibrational spiritual level.

All publications are available from Amazon online, and all publications, DVD and CDs are in Angel and Holistic centres around the country, as specified on Eileen's website: www.celestialhealing8.co.uk

Eileen is currently working on her fifteenth book, 'MUSIC OF THE SPHERES: Connecting to the Great Universal Consciousness through the musical compositions of Irish composer / pianist Pat McCourt'.

NOTE TO READER

Please note, that in keeping with modern scholarly designations in dating, I have used throughout this book C.E. instead of A.D. and B.C.E. instead of B.C.

C.E. means **Common Era** and refers to the years from the beginning of the first century onwards to modern times. **B.C.E.** means **Before the Common Era** and refers to the years before the first century.

Also, for the sake of clarity, I have referred to the canonical gospels just simply as Matthew, Mark, Luke and John, even though those gospels were not written by those particular named persons. These are just the names by which we know and recognise them.

And speaking of names! **Jesus** is the name presented to us in the gospels and in all Church teachings, and it is by that name that we recognise him. However, that is the Romanised version of his real name, attached to him by the Council of Nicaea in 325 C.E., all other names being declared heresy. Jesus' real name, the name by which he was known when he lived on earth 2000 years ago, was **Yeshua,** Yeshua ben Joseph, Yeshua son of Joseph. I have used both names throughout this book, and in no particular pattern, just to remind the reader that Yeshua was the real name. At the same time, however, it matters not in the Spirit world what name anyone goes by in this earth dimension. A name is only a label, an identification marker, for this earth plane only. In Spirit, names are irrelevant. There, it is all thought processing. Yeshua, known to us as Jesus, is now known to us **as Ascended Master Sananda** in the higher planes.

The **Essene Brotherhood,** that secretive and mysterious sect of

Judaism, to whom Jesus belonged, are not mentioned in the canonical gospels under that name. You will find them referred to as **Nazoreans**, a branch of the Essenes, just like the **Ebionites,** or the **Therapeutae,** this latter mostly near Alexandria in Egypt. Hence, contrary to widespread belief, **Jesus the Nazorean** does not mean **Jesus from Nazareth,** but **Jesus the Nazarene, Jesus the Essene.** He is sometimes referred to in the canonical gospels as **the Nazarene**

Capital letters have been used throughout to symbolise the specific, as distinct from the generic. For example, spiritual, church, bishop, pope, gospels, gods, doctrines, in general do not warrant a capital letter, but when spoken of in the specific, as for example, the Roman Christian Church, the Gospel of Philip, the Crucifixion of Jesus, then a capital letter is warranted.

The main texts used for the purpose of this book are the four **Canonical Gospels** in the New Testament. I am aware that there are many and diverse versions of the Bible, but the text I have used is the **Sunrise Good News Bible,** published by The Bible Societies / Collins. I have not altered in any way, but have quoted verbatim from this particular version. It is the writings in these canonical gospels that I am questioning, for their authenticity, their reliability and their validity, as they are the **main Christian** texts we have which claim that Jesus died on the cross and was resurrected three days later.

Other texts give us a very different story. Of these, the further texts I have included are suppressed gospels and epistles, in particular the **Gospel of Peter** and the **Gospel of Nicodemus.**

Also '**The Acts of Pilate',** ancient records recorded by contemporaries of Jesus regarding the facts concerning his birth, death and resurrection. Originally titled '**The Archko Volume**', translated by

Drs. McIntosh and Twyman, edited by Rev. W.D. Mahan, and published by Impact Christian Books, 332 Leffingwell Avenue, Kirkwood, MO 63122

I have also referred to '**The Crucifixion, by an Eye-Witness'**, a letter written seven years after the Crucifixion, by a personal friend of Jesus in Jerusalem, to an Essene Brother in Alexandria, published in 1915 by Chicago Indo-American Book Co./ 5705 South Boulevard.

Of all the modern research and recent writings now available, I have referred to **'The Essenes: Children of the Light'**, by Joanna Prentis and Stuart Wilson, a series of past-life regressions where those under regression could not possibly have known anything about what they revealed, and remembered nothing afterwards about what they had just disclosed.

ACKNOWLEDGEMENTS

I wish to thank, yet again, my publishers, Don Hale OBE and Dr. Steve Green for their patience, advice and input.

And my sincere thanks, yet again, to my family and my wonderful friends for their constant support and encouragement. You all know who you are!

Sincere and heart-felt appreciation to all of you who are buying my books and CDs and for your kind comments.

Thank you to all who attend my workshops and courses, and to all who have taken the time to write reviews for me, both in my books and on Amazon. You are greatly appreciated!

And as always, I give thanks for all the wonderful blessings that are constantly being bestowed upon us in this wonderful, loving, abundant Universe.

Namaste!

Eileen McCourt

3rd May, 2018

REVIEW

In Eileen McCourt's most recent work, 'Resurrection or Resuscitation, she turns her laser vision upon one of the most fundamental elements within Christianity, that Jesus was crucified, died and transcended death to rise on the third day. McCourt's credo in all her books, is that we have an ethical responsibility to question. To question is to gain understanding and understanding is the route to belief, or indeed disbelief, but certainly to truth. Whatever the result, it is a conclusion based on honesty and integrity. As McCourt points out, this is not a process that is promoted by the hierarchy of the Christian Church. This, in itself, should promote unease amongst its members.

In 'Resurrection and Resuscitation', McCourt clearly highlights some very pertinent questions that many theologians have dismissed. In a thorough and enlightening analysis, McCourt suggests that there are stunning historical inconsistencies and religious inaccuracies in the Church's version of events. Appropriately, McCourt places these personalities and their supposed actions within the context of the social, political and religious framework of the 'Holy Land' at the time of Jesus. In many instances, this story does not hold water when taken into account amongst the ritualistic practices of both the Jewish people, the Romans and the Essenes at the time of Jesus. When seen in this light, we notice that a very inexact picture comes to light. Are we missing some fundamental information? Was there a much deeper conspiracy amongst the main players? The reader must decide.

McCourt has highlighted some very pertinent and important questions for members of the Christian Church. Questions which they must ask to establish a realistic and consistent picture of Jesus Christ and the Church which they espouse. 'Resurrection or Resuscitation' is a stimulating and analytical work that suggests that the accepted story of Jesus' resurrection is, at best, glaringly inaccurate, at worst, a total fabrication of events. It would appear, however, that the road to truth, especially in relation to Jesus Christ, is not a straight one.

Declan Quigley

Declan Quigley is a Shamanic Practitioner, tutor, writer and founder of Anam Nasca Shamanism Ireland. He runs workshops, training seminars and healing clinics throughout Ireland and beyond. Contact Declan at <u>anamnasca@gmail.com</u> for more information.

FOREWORD

Those who are ready for this book, as with all my previous books, will no doubt find it. So if you have this book in your hands, you are ready. Ready for what? Ready for the challenge to step outside the restrictive boundaries of controlling religious dogmas and teachings, ready to think outside the box of blind faith, ready to take back responsibility for your own spiritual development.

Indeed, you may already be well on your way along your own spiritual path, well on your way along your own journey of spiritual enlightenment, well on your way to raising your own spiritual consciousness, and this book may simply be what you need at this point in time to clarify that you are not on your own, to reassure you that you are not alone in your thinking.

A great spiritual awakening is taking place right now, here on our Planet Earth, a great upward shift in spiritual consciousness, a great raising of the collective spiritual consciousness of all humanity such as has never happened before. Yes, the great Renaissance movement of the Medieval period in history, with all its characteristic questionings, challengings and explorations certainly produced a great upward shift. But the main difference in then and now is that religious institutions no longer exert the same suffocating influence and control over men's lives as they did then. Men like Copernicus or Galileo to name but a few, all suffered for their beliefs, teachings and scientific findings. Findings which have now long been accepted as the truth, but at the time were regarded as heresy, their exponents condemned as heretics, ruthlessly and brutally punished by the long octopus arms of the so-called Roman Christian Church, whose total control and authority over life and death knew no bounds. Then there was Leonardo da Vinci, whom we now know hid many clues for us in his paintings, clues for us to discover and interpret, clues as to what he believed to be the truths or untruths about Church teachings and what is related in the canonical gospels, all of which he was unable to write about openly, for fear of Church reprisal.

This is 2018. A different time. A different setting. A different way of looking at things. The Church no longer dictates medical advances. Church dogmas and teachings no longer dictate scientific thinking. The Church no longer holds the monopoly on literacy and education. The Church can no longer prevent us from exploring and questioning for ourselves.

And just like the early explorers who, in setting out to discover and experience the world for themselves, rather than relying, in blind faith, on the words of the ancient masters, discovered that the world was in fact, not flat at all, as those ancient masters had taught, so now, we too, in exploring and investigating the teachings and dogmas of the Church for ourselves, are discovering that these same long-held teachings and dogmas are seriously flawed, seriously unreliable in the truth department, and therefore for many people, no longer tenable.

2000 years is a long time in earthly reckoning. Can we ever know for certain what exactly happened back then? John Fitzgerald Kennedy was shot only half a century ago, and we still do not know the exact details concerning that, with all the cover-ups and conspiracy theories abounding. So how can we know for certain what happened 2000 years ago? The answer is, we just cannot!

But! And it is a big but! We can question and challenge that which we have always been led to believe actually happened!

Like many of my previous books, this book too is about questioning and challenging. I do not claim to have the answers, but I have the right to question and challenge, and that is what I am encouraging my readers to do. And that can only be a good thing if it exposes untruths for what they are and at the same time unearths the truth.

Did Jesus really die on the cross? Was there really a resurrection as the canonical gospels tell us? That is what this book attempts to investigate, and to separate the truth from the fiction.

The answer is either a simple yes or no. It cannot be both. The whole teachings of Christianity either rest or fall on the truth or the untruth of the death of Jesus on the cross and his subsequent resurrection. And if it were ever exposed that Jesus did not die on the cross, and therefore there could not possibly have been any resurrection, or indeed, if Jesus' tomb or his human remains were ever to be found, that would surely toll the death knell for entire Christianity as we have known it for almost two millennia.

So to re-emphasise a point! This book is not necessarily about PROVING anything. Rather, it is about questioning and challenging the story of the death, burial and resurrection of Jesus as related in the gospels and whether it is reliable. We can no longer ignore the need to question and challenge what is written in the canonical gospels! Those same gospels which are the foundation stone of the Roman Christian Church teachings!

It is surely an amazing fact that the vast majority of people throughout the world who profess to be Christians and followers of

Jesus, have never actually read these same gospels!

And an equally amazing fact is that of all those people who accept that the gospels are mostly metaphorical in nature, many still believe that the events related in those same gospels all actually happened!

The stark and indisputable fact is that no one actually *saw* the resurrection!

The resurrection is purely a matter of blind faith! And we know how blind faith tends to make fools of us all!

So I am, therefore, asking that you read this book with an open mind and an open heart. The frontiers of the impossible and the incredible are continuously and rapidly receding in our world today. And I am very conscious of the responsibility those of us must bear, those of us who strive to push back those very same boundaries.

Nevertheless, I make no apology. The truth must come out! The truth must be revealed! The truth must be made known to all! And all I am doing is adding one more burning stick to the already well built-up bonfire of untruths! Adding one more stone to the already well built-up edifice of untruths!

Much has been written over recent years to challenge the historicity of biblical accounts, and this is as it should be. It is only right that texts on which millions of people around the world base their faith should indeed be tested and questioned.

And this book, like all such books that challenge long-held beliefs, is of course open to ridicule and criticism. This matters little; it is of no consequence. I have written it in sincerity and honesty, and with my heart.

And I hope that your heart will be open enough to accept it! Open enough to accept that many of the movers and shapers of history have led us astray for their own devious and mercenary purposes.

It is time to expose what we have always been led to believe as being the irrefutable truth for what it really is! Unreliable and unsubstantiated! And definitely not irrefutable!

It is time for us to open our eyes and see for ourselves what is and what is not there!

And in so challenging and investigating, who knows what we will find? Certainly, at the very least, a lot for enthusiastic discussion!

Let us see!

CHAPTER 1:

The world into which Jesus was born

Jesus was born into first century Jewish Palestine, home to the Jewish religion Judaism. Jewish Palestine, a smouldering cauldron of political and social unrest and dissent. A Jewish Palestine torn apart by the religious and political power of the Pharisees and the Sadducees on the one hand and the political and military power of the Romans on the other. A Jewish Palestine awash not just with bandits and insurgent groups such as the Zealots, but also with messianic prophets declaring that the time of God's intervention to save his chosen people the Israelites, from the oppression of the hated Romans, was imminent.

A Jewish people steeped in superstition and a belief in a punishing, vindictive God who demanded constant appeasement through blood sacrifices. A Jewish people whose entire lives were centered around the goings-on in the Temple, controlled by the corrupt high priest and his cronies, who all profited handsomely from the vast amount of money that exchanged hands in the selling of sacrificial animals and the busy commerce that went on in the Temple courtyards on a daily basis, increasing immeasurably during the great feasts of Passover, when large numbers of Jews from all over the known world gathered in the great Temple in Jerusalem.

A Jewish people, for whose souls and bodies the Sanhedrin, the Jewish legislature, legislated. The Jewish Sanhedrin, for whom their religion and their politics were one and the same. The Jewish

Sanhedrin, who made the agreement with Caesar that the Jews were to pay a tax to the Romans, in return for which the Romans were not to interfere with the Jewish religion. An agreement which took the executive power out of the hands of the Jews and into the hands of the Romans. Hence the reason why Jesus was sent to Pontius Pilate to be condemned.

That agreement with the Romans that burdened the Jewish people with an onerous, oppressive and excessive system of taxation that kept money flowing into the Roman coffers. This, and the enforcement of offensive Roman standards and flags, the worst of which was the symbol of Roman power, the eagle, perched on the Temple in Jerusalem, dominating their city and seen for miles around, all added to the unrest among the Jewish people and increased their hatred of the oppressive foreign Romans.

Jewish society was divided up into numerous sects, the most important being the Sadducees and the Pharisees. Then there was the secretive sect of the Essenes, that sect of Judaism to which Jesus, his parents, Mary Magdalene and John the Baptist all belonged. I explained in a previous book, '*Jesus Lost and Found*' how this secretive Essene sect and the Essene communities scattered throughout Jewish Palestine and Egypt were a vital part of the story of the life of Jesus and his ministry. I showed how the Essenes spawned, birthed and raised Jesus, known as Yeshua, preparing him for his mission in fulfilling the ancient prophecies concerning the imminent arrival of a Messiah who would free the Jewish people from the hated Romans and restore God's Kingdom on earth.

And those prophecies foretold that the Messiah would be crucified and die on the cross for all mankind. Jesus was tailored by the Essenes to fulfil that role, a lamb to the slaughter.

But now it is time for us to turn our minds to the chief source that we have concerning the death and resurrection of Jesus, - *the canonical gospels.*

CHAPTER 2:

The Canonical Gospels

The Resurrection of Jesus is, for many people, the point at which Jesus the man becomes Jesus the God-man. Up until the resurrection, we see the historical Jesus, the Jesus on whom we can put some flesh and bones. But that is the end of Jesus as a human. From the resurrection onwards, Jesus becomes the Jesus of faith, Jesus the supernatural, untouchable, unfathomable, unsubstantiated.

In one of my previous books, *'The Almost Immaculate Deception'*, I pointed out how Jesus, in dying on the cross and being resurrected from the dead, was not at all unique. Numerous Roman and Greek gods also attained immortality in the same way, all born on December 25th, just after the winter solstice when the sun begins its ascent once more, all performing miracles, all dying to atone for the sins of mankind, and all being resurrected from the dead after three days. Yes, Jesus' C.V. is exactly the same as that of many Greek and Roman gods!

I pointed out too, how the early Christian Church fathers needed a god-man image in order to compete with other religions and beliefs of the time, and when the Roman Emperor Constantine, in the early fourth century, declared the Christian religion to be the one and only religion of the Roman Empire, it was the historical figure of Jesus, healer and teacher, on whom this new God image was super-imposed, and they manipulated and distorted the truth in order to fulfil their purpose, placating a superstitious people by furthering the image of an angry, punishing, vengeful, male God. And all in order to exert and maintain control and to bring some sort of common identity and cohesion to the vast sprawling Roman empire.

In fact, what they did was by-pass the teachings of Jesus, ignore all his criticisms of the political and religious leaders of his society, and re-instate and strengthen all that Jesus had tried to change about Jewish beliefs during his ministry. It was almost as if Jesus had never existed at all. Yes, Christianity had its origins in Jewish Judaism! Not with Jesus!

No other religion, apart from the Roman Christian religion, proclaims that Jesus died on the cross and was resurrected from death three days later, thereby redeeming mankind from sin and securing for us eternal life. That Jesus died in appeasement for our sins and the sins of all mankind, is the message that has been promulgated by the Roman Christian Church since the early fourth century, since Christianity as a declared religion began. And because of that, we are told, we can now enjoy salvation and eternal life. All we have to do is believe and follow the teachings and dogmas laid down by the Church, obey the rules without questioning, and we will automatically get a pass into heaven.

But Jesus did not wish to found a new religion or establish a new Church. His one intention was to reform what was already there, to change the beliefs of the Jewish people from the crippling religion that kept them steeped in fear and superstition, chained to a corrupt, greedy and power hungry priestly class who paraded themselves through an elaborate temple system and constant flamboyant ceremonies, setting themselves up as the only intermediaries between all people and God. Jesus attempted to stir up the volatile pot of tradition, adding to it the teachings he had absorbed from the many diverse cultures in his travels to other countries, during those *'missing years'*, those years left unaccounted for in the canonical gospels.

Jesus and his disciples were not known as Christians. Jesus was teaching '*The Way*' and his followers were known as '*Followers of the Way*'. And when we compare the teachings of the Roman Christian Church with the teachings of Jesus, we can clearly see that Christianity as we know it, is definitely NOT founded on those teachings of Jesus!

The chief place we find the story of Jesus' death, burial and resurrection is in the four canonical gospels, believed by those who profess to be Christians, to be the foundation stone of the teachings of the Roman Christian Church. Historians and writers of that time and the early centuries, do not tell us anything like what the four canonical gospels tell us. Their silence speaks volumes! And that alone should have rung alarm bells for us long ago!

In a previous book, '...*And that's the Gospel Truth*', I pointed out that the gospels are not historical documents, and should not be treated as such. They are flawed, unreliable and unsubstantiated. They are littered with inconsistencies, historical inaccuracies, interpolations and contradictions. And rather than accept what we have always been led to believe, that we have four separate, independent and individual accounts, when we read them, we can clearly see that this is, in fact, not at all the case.

The first written gospel, contrary to what we have always been led to believe, was not Matthew, but Mark. Mark's Gospel, written in 70 C.E. provides us with the basic narrative framework of the life of the man whom the gospels call Jesus of Nazareth. This in itself is a misnomer. He was Yeshua, Yeshua the Nazarene, the Nazarenes being a branch of the Essenes. But the gospels do not even mention the Essenes!

The second gospel was written ten years after Mark, 80-85 C.E. and for the most part, the writer of this gospel uses Mark as his main source. So we have what is mostly a repeat of the original Mark. The third gospel, Luke, was written 85-90 C.E. and the writer of this gospel follows the same pattern, to a great extent, as the two former gospels, changing some material and adding some of his own. Finally, the Gospel of John was written, 90-100 or so C.E., and is more theologically orientated, offering us an entirely different version, focusing more on Jesus the Divine and exalted Son of God. It would appear that when the end of the world or the apocalypse did not materialise as the first three gospels said would happen, then the story was changed in the fourth gospel. Hence we have a new Jesus, a Jesus hardly recognisable from the previous three gospels.

So, when we boil it all down, we are left with not four different versions, but just two different versions, the first three gospels being known as the 'synoptic' gospels, meaning 'from the same view point', or 'from one identical source', and the third gospel, that of John, written in Ephesus, towards the end of the first century C.E., being at variance with the previous three, and considered by many to be the most authentic of all the four narratives.

These then are the first written narratives of the life of Jesus. Before this, all teachings were passed down orally, as was the custom in the Ancient Mystery Schools, most probably to prevent such important information from falling into the hands of the wrong people. These Ancient Mystery Schools, what they taught, and their importance in the life of Jesus, I have covered in depth in a previous book, '*Jesus Lost and Found: Resurrected for real 2000 years later*'.

Information and narratives handed down orally through time do indeed tend to become embellished to a large degree. A bit like Chinese whispers!

But that is not the only problem with the canonical gospels!

We do not actually know who these four writers were. Matthew, Mark, Luke and John are mere pseudo names, as was the custom at that time. Nor do we have the original scripts, which were written in Greek, while Jesus and his disciples are known to have spoken Aramaic. The writers of the gospels were highly educated, highly literate and skilled, and not what we would expect from the lower classes of society at that time, such as poor fishermen, who would have been illiterate and uneducated. Furthermore, when we look at the dates of the writing of these four gospels, we can clearly see that these writers could not have been the disciples of Jesus, because according to the gospels, Jesus died at 33 years of age, so this Matthew, Mark, Luke and John, whoever they actually were, could not have been around Jesus. Therefore, what we have been led to believe were eye-witness accounts, and as such, sold to us as being reliable, cannot be eye-witness accounts at all. There is no first person narrative, no personal '*I*' or '*we*', only the remote third person narrative which distances the authors from their writings.

And it was these particular four gospels, re-edited numerous times, with all their inconsistencies and contradictions, that were named as the Canonical Gospels, the basis of the teachings of the Roman Christian Church, all other gospels and writings being banned and burned, their writers punished as heretics by a Roman Christian Church that tolerated no opposition whatsoever. A Roman Christian Church that inflicted pain, suffering and death on millions as history unfolded, and all in the name of Jesus. A Roman Christian Church that brought in dogma after dogma as the years progressed, none of which are to be found in any historical or theological literature of the early centuries.

Not at all Jesus-like, one could most certainly say!

And a further major point which needs to be emphasised! Those Christians who have actually read the gospels must surely not have failed to have noticed the constant repetition of such phrases throughout as '*This was said in order to fulfil the prophecies*', and '*Jesus did this so that the prophecy might be fulfilled*'. Such phrases, constantly repeated again and again, can only lead us to believe that the stories related within those gospels are just that, - stories! Stories built up around the fulfilling of the prophecies in the Old Testament!

So where does all this leave us with regards to the gospels? Certainly not looking good for the reliability, the authenticity or the validity of them! And so many of those people around the world who profess to be Christians still consider them to be the truth!

I now want to take you further into what we are actually told about the death, burial and resurrection of Jesus, as narrated in those same canonical gospels. And I hope, when we scrutinise what we have been told in those same gospels, each reader will then be more able to decide for himself what is most likely to have happened in that tomb, or indeed, what is most likely to have NOT happened!

Resurrection or resuscitation?

CHAPTER 3:

Jewish burial customs 2000 years ago

Jesus was born into Jewish Palestine, and being a Jew, we would expect that he would be given a Jewish burial when he died. Right? So we need to first of all consider what a Jewish burial in the first century C.E. entailed. The Book of Numbers in the old Testament tells us about attitudes people had about touching dead bodies:

'Everyone who is unclean by contact with a corpse.' (Numbers 5:2)

'The priest shall offer one (pigeon) as a sin offering and the other as a burnt offering to perform the ritual of purification for them because of their contact with a corpse.' (Numbers 6:11)

'Whoever touches a corpse is ritually unclean for seven days. He must purify himself with the water for purification on the third day and on the seventh day, and then he will be clean. But if he does not purify himself on the third day and the seventh day, he will not be clean.....he will no longer be considered one of God's people.' (Numbers 19:11-13)

'If someone touches a person who has been killed or died a natural death out of doors or if someone touches a human bone or a grave he becomes unclean for seven days.' (Numbers 19:16)

We know that the early Egyptians embalmed their dead. Even the Old Testament refers to it:

'Joseph threw himself on his father, crying and kissing his face.

Then Joseph gave orders to embalm his father's body. It took 40 days, the normal time for embalming. The Egyptians mourned for him 70 days'. (Genesis 50:1-3)

'Joseph died in Egypt at the age of 110. They embalmed his body and put it in a coffin.' (Genesis 50:26)

But Jesus was not reported dead in Egypt! Jesus was reported dead in Jewish Palestine! The Mishnah, Judaism's first major canonical document following the Bible, and forming a basic part of the Talmud, tells us very clearly that there were three major stages to preparing the body for burial in the Jewish religion.

Ritual purification was strictly adhered to by the Jewish people as much in death as in everyday life. In fact, all evidence clearly confirms that they were obsessed with ritual purity!

So firstly, the eyes of the dead person were closed and the body washed carefully, thoroughly cleansed of all dirt, body fluids, and anything that might be on the skin. Any bleeding was stopped and all blood was buried with the deceased. The Book of Acts, reporting the death of Tabitha in Joppa also mentions the washing of her corpse as part of the burial preparations:

'Her body was washed and laid in a room upstairs'. (Acts 9:37)

Secondly, the body was purified and anointed with oils. Finally, as is mentioned in many Jewish sources, it was not just dressed, but wrapped and bound in shrouds, garments specially prepared or just freshly washed for the explicit purpose of wrapping the dead.

At the time of Jesus, in first century Jewish Palestine, the body was elaborately wrapped in such a shroud and the face was covered with a special cloth called a '*sudarium*'. The hands and feet were bound with strips of cloth.

We are also told that the preparation of the corpse for burial further included trimming the hair, the only exception being unmarried girls, who were buried with their hair loose, just as brides were brought to their wedding.

The Jews very seldom cremated their dead and only usually at the request for cremation by the dying person. Mostly, they avoided the practice of cremation as they believed in the resurrection of the body.

Burial was always very prompt, usually before sundown of the day of death, as Jewish law and custom specified immediate burial of a dead body. Mosaic law required that the body of a man put to death by hanging on a tree or a cross be buried the same day he died:

'If someone has been put to death for a crime and his body is hung on a post, it is not to remain there overnight. It must be buried the same day, because a dead body hanging on a post brings God's curse on the land.' (Deuteronomy 22:22-23)

The relatives and friends carried the corpse in a procession towards the place of burial, all the while mourning and wailing. Such a procession is mentioned in Luke's Gospel:

'Just as he arrived at the gate of the town, a funeral procession was coming out. The dead man was the only son of a woman who was a widow, and a large crowd from the town was with her.' (Luke 7:12)

And in Mark's Gospel, we read how the funeral preparations for Jairus' daughter began immediately:

'They arrived at Jairus' house, where Jesus saw the confusion and heard all the loud crying and wailing.' (Mark 5:38)

13

Burial places, or cemeteries, were to be at least fifty yards beyond any village or town. The typical Jewish tomb itself was hallowed out of the side of a rock. There would be a front part, known as the outer chamber, and a back part, known as the inner chamber. The body was deposited, lengthways, head first, on a shelf cut into the rock in the outer chamber. Then, after the final respects were completed, a large round stone was rolled into position to cover the tomb. These large stones were often whitewashed, possibly because the lime in the whitewash acted as a cleansing agent, a sort of disinfectant, and probably also to warn people passing by that this was in fact a burial site. This was important, because as we have seen earlier in this chapter, coming into contact with a dead person incurred ritual uncleanliness for at least seven days afterwards, and required ritual purification before that person could be considered clean again.

After about a year, family members would return to the tomb, collect the bones and place them in a box known as an '*ossuary*'. The box would be marked with some identification and placed in the back room of the tomb along with other relatives who had previously been buried there. That was important for Jewish people, to '*rest with their ancestors*'. We read in the Book of Genesis how Joseph, on his death bed in Egypt, asked his people:

'*Promise me that when God leads you to that (promised) land, you will take my body with you*'. (Genesis 50: 25)

Poor people who could not afford a rock-hewn tomb, or foreigners who were maybe just passing and had no land were buried within vertical shafts in designated fields. We read in Matthew's Gospel how, when Judas realised what he had done, he threw the money back at the chief priests and:

'*After reaching an agreement about it, they used the money to buy Potter's Field, as a cemetery for foreigners.*' (Matthew 27:7)

So these then were the usual customs observed at Jewish burials in Jewish Palestine at the time of Jesus in the first century.

Let us now consider the two burials we are told about in the canonical gospels - the burial of Lazarus and the burial of Jesus.

CHAPTER 4:

The burial of Lazarus

It is only in John's Gospel that we read about the death and burial of Lazarus, and then Jesus raising him from the dead. Such an event as someone being raised from the dead is certainly far from the norm, and yet no historian of the time tells of it, and no other gospel relates it! Why not? One can only speculate!

According to John's Gospel, Lazarus was well and truly dead. Whether, in reality, he was dead or not is another issue, and the very issue which I have already dealt with in a previous book, *'Behind Every Great Man........ Mary Magdalene Twin Flame of Jesus'*.

But whether Lazarus was actually dead or not is not important here. What is important is that Mary and Martha, the sisters of Lazarus, and all the others around them **believed** Lazarus to be dead. Hence they had buried him. And buried him very quickly, as was the Jewish custom, as we have seen in the previous chapter. Jesus delayed three days in getting there, and we are told:

'When Jesus arrived, he found that Lazarus had been buried four days before'. (John 11:17)

'Martha, the dead man's sister, answered, 'There will be a bad smell, Lord. He has been buried four days!'. (John 11:39)

So we can take it from this that Lazarus was buried very quickly, as was the Jewish custom.

Furthermore:

"*Jesus said, 'Our friend Lazarus has fallen asleep, but I will go and wake him up'. The disciples answered, 'If he is asleep, Lord, he will get well'.*

Jesus meant that Lazarus had died, but they thought he meant natural sleep. So Jesus told them plainly, 'Lazarus is dead, but for your sake I am glad that I was not with him, so that you will believe. Let us go to him'. "
(John 11:11-15)

"*Martha said to Jesus, 'If you had been here, Lord, my brother would not have died'.* " (John 11:21)

So Lazarus was most certainly **believed** to be well and truly dead. Otherwise they would surely not have buried him!

Next, John's Gospel tells us:

'*Jesus went to the tomb, which was a cave with a stone placed at the entrance. 'Take the stone away!' Jesus ordered.'*(John 11:38)

So here we have the cave with the stone at the entrance. All normal for a Jewish burial in first century Jewish Palestine.

'*Jesus called in a loud voice, 'Lazarus, come out!' Lazarus came out, his hands and feet wrapped in grave clothes, and with a cloth round his face.*' (John 11:44)

'*Untie him', Jesus told them, 'and let him go'.* (John 11: 44)

Again, we have the normal custom being followed, with Lazarus being wrapped in grave clothes. We can assume, surely, that his feet were bound too? Otherwise, why would Jesus have ordered him to be untied?

BUT! With his feet and his body wrapped up, needing others to untie him, how did Lazarus manage to come out of the cave on his own, without any help as the words 'Lazarus came out' suggests? He was obviously already out when Jesus ordered him to be untied! The only way he could have got out was if he hopped out! And if he had 'a cloth round his face', then how did he manage to breathe?

So, as we can see, there are just too many questions left unanswered! Credibility is being pushed to the extreme surely?

We learn nothing about how Lazarus' body was treated prior to the burial itself, but the few pieces of information we do get suggest that at least some of the customs appear to have been carried out. And that was because Lazarus was **believed to be actually dead**.

So for the purpose of this book, the important thing to remember is that Lazarus was **believed** to be dead, hence buried, and buried in the way we would expect at that time for a Jew in Jewish Palestine to be buried.

It is now time to consider how Jesus was buried!

CHAPTER 5:

The burial of Jesus

We have just seen, from the one and only gospel that relates the death, burial and raising of Lazarus, that Lazarus was indeed buried according to at least some of the burial customs of first century Jewish Palestine. And buried because he was **believed** to be really dead. His burial appears to have been indeed intended as a final interment.

Now it is time to look at how Jesus was buried, which is related in all four canonical gospels.

Were all the rites normally included in a burial in Jewish Palestine carried out in the burial of Jesus? Closing the eyes? Washing the body and anointing with oils? Trimming the beard and hair? Covering the face with a cloth, a sudarium? Binding the body in burial shrouds? Funeral procession? Burial in a cave cut out of the side of a rock? And placed on a shelf, lengthways, head first?

What do Mark, Matthew, Luke and John tell us about the burial of Jesus?

'Joseph bought a linen sheet, took the body down, wrapped it in the linen sheet, and placed it in a tomb which had been dug out of solid rock. Then he rolled a large stone across the entrance to the tomb.' (Mark 15:46)

'So Joseph took the body, wrapped it in a new linen sheet, and

placed it in his own tomb, which he had just recently dug out of solid rock. Then he rolled a large stone across the entrance to the tomb and went away.' (Matthew 27:59)

'Then Joseph took the body down, wrapped it in a linen sheet, and placed it in a tomb which had been dug out of solid rock and which had never been used.' (Luke 23:53)

'The two men (Joseph and Nicodemus) took Jesus' body and wrapped it in linen with the spices according to the Jewish custom of preparing a body for burial. There was a garden in the place where Jesus had been put to death, and in it there was a new tomb where no one had ever been buried. Since it was the day before the Sabbath and because the tomb was close by, they placed Jesus' body there.' (John 19:40-42)

So this is all we are told in the canonical gospels about the actual burial of Jesus.

There are only a few points on which all four agree. Firstly, they all agree that it was Joseph of Arimathea who took the body from the cross, and only John tells he was assisted by Nicodemus. Who was Joseph of Arimathea? Who was Nicodemus? We will consider both of these later, in a separate chapter.

Secondly, all four agree that Jesus was wrapped in a linen sheet.

Thirdly, all agree that the body was placed in a tomb which had never been used before. Matthew goes further and tells us the tomb was Joseph's own tomb.

But where was this tomb? The first three synoptic gospels tell us it was dug out of solid rock. Then John tells us it was in the garden in the place where Jesus had been put to death. So while the synoptic gospels tell us it was a rock tomb, John tells us it was a garden tomb.

Let us look deeper!

John tells us the body was wrapped in linen with the spices *'according to the Jewish custom of burial'*. We will consider the spices separately in a later chapter.

But *'according to the Jewish custom of burial'*?

We have already seen what the customs of a Jewish burial in first century Jewish Palestine entailed. Were these adhered to in the burial of Jesus?

First of all, no gospel mentions the body of Jesus being washed. Secondly, there is no mention of the body being anointed with oils. Thirdly, there is no mention of the body being bound in burial shrouds. So what could one conclude from this? That those who wrote these gospels did not know the rituals of a Jewish burial? How then could they have been with Jesus? How could they even have been from Jewish Palestine? Bearing in mind the gospels were written originally in Greek, and by very literate people, then it seems like the Roman Christian Church claim for authenticity of these gospels on the grounds of these writers actually being with Jesus cannot be accepted.

OR! Can we conclude that ***Jesus was not dead***? Unlike Lazarus who was truly believed to be dead?

And if Jesus was not actually dead, then would that not be a perfect explanation for Joseph not washing his body? Washing Jesus' body would have opened up all the wounds, sores and cuts again, renewing the profuse bleeding, the very thing Joseph and Nicodemus wanted to avoid and to make sure did not happen!

Indeed, as we have just seen, the gospels are remarkably silent on all of the Palestinian Jewish burial procedures. There is not even any description of the removal of Jesus from the cross. And bearing in mind how touching a dead body incurred uncleanliness for seven days, then who exactly took Jesus from the cross? Joseph of Arimathea could certainly not have managed it on his own, and not even with just Nicodemus helping him. He would have needed more help than just one other man to transport the body to the tomb, and especially since, as we shall see later, Nicodemus was already carrying a large heavy weight of spices!

And then there is the question of the new tomb, supposed to be for Joseph of Arimathea himself, but now conveniently and coincidentally placed very near the place of Jesus' crucifixion. Add to this the curious and unusually large amount of spices and herbs which John tells us were brought to the tomb by Nicodemus, one of the chief healers in the Essenes community; the centurion who lanced the side of Jesus with his spear instead of allowing his soldiers to break Jesus' legs, as was the custom; the drink administered to Jesus, which caused him to expire immediately; the *loud voice* in which Jesus was able to cry out, despite his struggle to even breathe, and the short duration of time he was left on the cross. And then later there is the question about Pilate's surprise when told that Jesus was dead; the rolled-away stone at the tomb entrance; the confusion over who actually first saw the empty tomb, and Mary Magdalene's puzzling words *'They have taken my Lord away and I do not know where they have put him'.* (John 20:13)

Serious questions surround all of these. Questions which we need to ask!

We will now consider each in a separate chapter, beginning with Joseph of Arimathea and that new tomb, whether a rock tomb or a garden tomb.

CHAPTER 6:

Joseph of Arimathea and the new tomb

Who was Joseph of Arimathea? Some sources tell us he was the uncle of Jesus, being the brother of Jesus' mother Mary. Other sources tell us he was the great-uncle of Jesus, being the uncle of Jesus' mother Mary.

Whichever version is correct, we can be certain that he was indeed an important member of the immediate family of Jesus and an important force in his life.

What else do we know about him?

We know he was very powerful and held great influence in Jewish Palestine. His vast tin mining operations in Cornwall and Devon assured him privileges with the Romans, his vast fleet of ships plying back and forth across the Mediterranean and beyond to Britain, known then as Avalon, bringing back vast amounts of the metal tin for the making of weapons for the rapidly expanding Roman armies. And we know that Jesus accompanied him on several journeys to Avalon, to the ancient mystery schools there.

And unknown to the Roman or Jewish authorities, Joseph was a member of the secretive Essene community, of which Jesus, his parents and Mary Magdalene were also members. His grand houses were scattered throughout Jewish Palestine, affording shelter, respite and protection to other Essenes.

He was also a member of the Sanhedrin, the Jewish legislative party. And as such, he had access to vital and confidential inside information.

'The Crucifixion by an eye-witness' a letter from an Essene Brother in Jerusalem to another Essene Brother in Alexandria, just seven years after the Crucifixion, tells us:

'There was a certain Joseph, from Arimathea. He was rich, and being a member of the council, he was much esteemed by the people. He was a prudent man, and whilst he did not appear to belong to any party, he was secretly a member of our sacred Order and lived in accordance with our laws.'

So Joseph was an Essene! AND a member of the council of the Sanhedrin, the Jewish ruling authorities!

And as a member of the Essene community, he would have known all about the destiny of Jesus as the Messiah, and the fate that awaited him. The prophecies foretold that Jesus was to be crucified and die on the cross, and then be resurrected after three days. Joseph, as a member of the Sanhedrin, was very much at the centre of the hub of political activity, and very much at the nerve centre of the goings-on around the crucifixion itself.

A very powerful man indeed!

And what do the gospels tell us about this same Joseph of Arimathea?

'He was a respected member of the Council, who was waiting for the Kingdom of God.' (Mark 15:42)

'When it was evening, a rich man from Arimathea arrived; his name

was Joseph, and he also was a disciple of Jesus.' (Matthew 27:57)

'There was a man named Joseph from Arimathea, a town in Judea. He was a good and honourable man, who was waiting for the Kingdom of God. Although he was a member of the Council, he had not agreed with their decision and action. He went into the presence of Pilate and asked for the body of Jesus.' (Luke 23:50-52)

'After this, Joseph who was from the town of Arimathea, asked Pilate if he could take Jesus' body. (Joseph was a follower of Jesus, but in secret, because he was afraid of the Jewish authorities.) Pilate told him he could have the body, so Joseph went and took it away.' (John 19:38)

Again, we can ask the question, did these gospel writers really know much about him? If they did not know he was an Essene? Or related to Jesus?

The answer? Obviously not! Reminding us, yet again, that those writers could not have been anywhere near the scenes of all the action!

We saw in the last chapter how all the gospels tell us that the tomb in which Jesus was laid had never been used before, and Matthew goes further and tells us it was Joseph's own tomb. But why would Joseph have his own tomb so near the place where Jesus was crucified? And why did it just manifest so shortly before the crucifixion?

Let us draw all this information together now and see what logical conclusion we can come to about Joseph of Arimathea.

Being on the inside of all the activity of the Sanhedrin and of the Essenes leading up to the crucifixion, which Joseph would certainly have known was going to happen, is it not logical to conclude that the tomb in the garden was not at all for Joseph himself, but for Jesus, and it needed to be near the crucifixion site itself, in order to get Jesus off the cross and into a place of safety and healing as quickly as possible?

Certainly, everything about Joseph's actions and the part he played strongly suggest that the burial of Jesus in that tomb was not a final interment! That tomb was constructed specially for the body of Jesus! A Jesus who was not in fact dead, but needed to appear dead in order to fulfil the prophecies, and to appear dead in order to get the Jewish authorities off his back because otherwise, if they thought he was still alive, they would go after him again, and make sure the process was finished properly!

What better way to keep Jesus safe than to place him in the tomb of a person believed to be dead? And bearing in mind how the Jewish people were reticent to come into contact with a dead body, then Jesus would have been safe from prying eyes!

It appears that Joseph had instigated a master plan that swung into operation before Jesus was actually crucified! A plan that would rescue him from death on the cross. Jesus could not escape the crucifixion itself, but he could be rescued from the jaws of death!

But this all came at a cost for Joseph of Arimathea!

'Joseph and Nicodemus beseeched Jesus that he save himself and not again permit himself to fall into the power of the priests. Joseph even told him that it had come to him that Caiaphas had

fixed his suspicions upon him, that he, too, with the Galileans, formed a secret plot to overthrow the present conditions of things, and that Caiaphas would demand of him an explanation why he had laid Jesus in his own tomb.' (The Crucifixion by an eye-witness)

The past-life regressionists Stuart Wilson and Joanna Prentis, in their book, **'The Essenes: Children of the Light'** also confirm that Joseph of Arimathea was himself a marked man after the crucifixion:

'By the time the Pharisees finally got authorization to open and inspect the tomb, the work had been completed and nothing suspicious could be found. As usual, the Brotherhood had covered its tracks efficiently, and by then Jesus had been taken to Qumran and thence from one safe house to another north to Damascus.

Joseph's interventions to obtain the body of Jesus, and later to keep the tomb closed, cost him dearly. These were the first times he had spoken publicly for any Essene, as up to then all had been done quietly behind the scenes. From that point on, people began asking where Joseph's real loyalty lay. When the Pharisees found nothing amiss in the tomb their full fury turned upon Joseph and he realized that he would very soon have to leave. If all traces of Jesus had eluded them, at least they had the living Joseph to vent their rage upon. From that time all the weight of their investigations centered upon Joseph and his connections with the Essenes.' (The Essenes: Children of the Light', Joanna Prentis and Stuart Wilson, page 174)

Now it is time to turn our sights on Joseph's accomplice, Nicodemus!

CHAPTER 7:

Nicodemus and the spices

Who was Nicodemus? Nicodemus who appears only at the crucifixion, assisting Joseph of Arimathea. From where did he suddenly appear?

The gospels do not tell us much! No surprise there! And, as always, what they do tell us needs to be questioned! No surprise there either!

Neither Mark nor Matthew nor Luke mention Nicodemus. It is only from John that we hear about him. John refers to him several times:

"There was a Jewish leader named Nicodemus, who belonged to the party of the Pharisees. One night he went to Jesus and said to him, 'Rabbi, we know that you are a teacher sent by God. No one could perform the miracles you are doing unless God were with him'. " (John 3:1-2)

'Nicodemus, who at first had gone to see Jesus at night'. (John 19:39)

This clearly suggests that Nicodemus was initiated in some way by Jesus in a secret meeting by night. We know from other sources, such as the writings on past-life regressions of Dolores Cannon, Joanna Prentis and Stuart Wilson that Nicodemus was indeed one of the highest level of healers in the secretive Essene community, and also a Jewish councillor. But the gospels make absolutely no mention at all of the Essene community! That Essene sect of the Jewish people to whom Jesus, his parents, Mary Magdalene, and John the Baptist all belonged! Did those who wrote these gospels not know about the Essenes?

And according to John, Jesus himself calls Nicodemus *'a great teacher in Israel'.* (John 3:10)

There are other texts however, which throw further light on Nicodemus!

'The Crucifixion, by an eye-witness', a letter written seven years after the Crucifixion, by a personal friend of Jesus in Jerusalem to an Essene brother in Alexandria, tells us:

'Joseph's friend Nicodemus was a most learned man, and belonged to the highest degrees of our Order. He knew the secrets of the 'Terapeuts' and was often together with us.'

The **'Terapeuts'** referred to here were the Egyptian branch of the Essenes, highly skilled in the art and practice of healing.

'The Gospel of Nicodemus' is one of the suppressed gospels and epistles, one of those that never found its way into the canonical gospels. This pseudepigraphal Gospel of Nicodemus was appended to the apocryphal Acts of Pilate and gives us further insight into who this man Nicodemus was:

"But Nicodemus, a certain Jew / stood before the governor, / and said, 'I entreat thee, / O righteous judge, that thou / wouldst favour me with the / liberty of speaking a few words.' / Pilate said to him,

'Speak on'. / Nicodemus said, 'I spake to / the elders of the Jews, and the / scribes, and priests and Levites, / and all the multitude of the Jews, / in their assembly; What is it ye / would do with this man? / He is a man who hath wrought many useful and glorious miracles, / such as no man on earth ever / wrought before, nor will ever / work. Let him go, and do him / no harm; if he cometh from God, / his miracles (his miraculous cures) will continue; but if from / men, they will come to nought. / Thus Moses, when he was / sent by God into Egypt, wrought / the miracles which God commanded / him, before Pharaoh of Egypt; /and though the magicians of that / country, Jannes and Jambres, / wrought by their magic the same / miracles which Moses did, yet they / could not work all which he did; / And the miracles which the / magicians wrought, were not of / God, as ye know, O Scribes and / Pharisees; but they who wrought / them perished, and all who / believed them. / And now let this man go; / because the very miracles for / which ye accuse him, are from God; and he is not worthy of / death'. The Jews then said to Nicodemus, / 'Art thou become his disciple, / and making speeches in his favour?' Nicodemus said to them, 'Is /the governor become his disciple / also, and does he make speeches / for him? Did not Caesar place / him in that high post?' / When the Jews heard this / they trembled, and gnashed their / teeth at Nicodemus, and said to / him, 'Mayest thou receive his / doctrine for truth, and have thy lot with Christ!' / Nicodemus replied, 'Amen; / I will receive his doctrine, and / my lot with him, as ye have said'."
(Gospel of Nicodemus 5:1-11)

So we can clearly see that Nicodemus was a staunch follower and defender of Jesus, fearless indeed, in the face of Jewish opposition:

"But when they all concealed / themselves through fear of the / Jews , Nicodemus alone showed / himself to them, and said, 'How / can such persons as these enter / into the synagogue?' / The Jews answered him, 'But how durst thou enter into the / synagogue, who wast a confederate / with Christ? Let thy lot be along / with him in the other world'./ Nicodemus answered, ' Amen / so may it be, that I may have / my lot with him in his Kingdom'. " (Gospel of Nicodemus 9:3-4)

However, Nicodemus' chief claim to fame or indeed, even for recognition, is the spices and herbs he brought to the scene of the Crucifixion. In the same Gospel of Nicodemus we read:

'And Nicodemus came, bringing / with him a mixture of myrrh and / aloes, about a hundred pounds / weight; and they took down Jesus/ from the cross with tears, and / bound him in linen cloths with spices'. (Gospel of Nicodemus 8: 14)

And in the Gospel of John:

'Nicodemus went with Joseph, taking with him about 30 kilogrammes of spices, a mixture of myrrh and aloes. The two men took Jesus' body, and wrapped it in linen with the spices according to the Jewish custom of preparing a body for burial.' (John 19:39-40)

But why does John write *'according to the Jewish custom of preparing a body for burial'* while at the same time describing a burial which was NOT in accordance with the Jewish custom? The body of Jesus should have been washed and anointed with oils, before being wrapped in clean burial shrouds! But instead, according to John, it was *'wrapped'* with spices! What was

Nicodemus doing wrapping Jesus with spices? Spices and herbs were for medicinal purposes, to heal wounds! But why would one try to heal wounds on a dead body?

Jesus was obviously not dead!

In fact, in **'The Crucifixion by an Eye-witness'**, we read that it was Nicodemus who declared Jesus to be still alive:

"When Nicodemus saw the wound, flowing with water and blood, his eyes were animated with new hope, and he spoke encouragingly, foreseeing what was to happen.

He drew Joseph aside to where I stood, some distance from John, and spoke in a low, hurried tone: 'Dear friends, be of good cheer, and let us to work. Jesus is not dead. He seems so only because his strength is gone....... But I admonish you that you tell not John we hope to reanimate the body of Jesus, lest he could not conceal his great joy. And dangerous indeed would it be if the people should come to know it, for our enemies would then put us all to death with him'. "

Here we have the clear hint that secrecy was the key to it all!

And again, from that same source:

"Joseph and Nicodemus examined the body of Jesus, and Nicodemus, greatly moved, drew Joseph aside and said to him: 'As sure as is my knowledge of life and nature, so sure is it possible to save him'. But Joseph did not understand him and he admonished us that we should not tell John of what we had heard. Indeed, it was a secret which was to save our Brother from death.

*Nicodemus shouted: 'We must immediately have the body with its bones unbroken, because he may still be saved'; then, realizing his want of caution, he continued in a whisper, 'saved from being infamously buried'. (*The Crucifixion by an Eye-witness)

So we have two stories being put out! The story of Jesus being dead, put out to the people for fear of reprisal from the Jews, and the story held in secret by the Essenes! The secret story of the survival of Jesus! The secret story that **Jesus was not dead**!

But let us return to the spices! In particular, the amount of spices and herbs Nicodemus had with him. 30 kilogrammes is a lot! Roughly about 75-100 Roman pounds! A heavy weight to carry! Even the short distance from the site of crucifixion to that new garden tomb which we have already ascertained Joseph constructed specially for the body of Jesus! More men would certainly have been needed to help carry both the body of Jesus and the heavy weight of spices. Joseph of Arimathea and Nicodemus on their own could not have done it. And the canonical gospels do not relate how Jesus was taken from the cross. Such a delicate and important operation is totally missing! We are only told that the body was taken from the cross, but we are told nothing about HOW it was taken from that cross. Surely it would have been a specialist task? Extracting the nails? Holding the body? But we are told nothing!

In the first century, myrrh was obtained from Arabia, Abyssinia and India, carried along the trade routes by caravans of camels to the Mediterranean ports. Such a large amount as what Nicodemus had would have been gathered up over a period of time, and not just acquired a day or two before the crucifixion.

So Nicodemus must have known he was going to need a lot of healing spices for Jesus. And he was well prepared beforehand. Just like Joseph of Arimathea was well prepared beforehand with the new garden tomb, supposedly for himself, and conveniently placed near the crucifixion site, so too, Nicodemus was well prepared with a large amount of healing herbs and spices.

'Thereupon, Nicodemus spread strong spices and healing salves on long pieces of 'byssus' which he had brought, and whose use was known only in our Order.

These he wound about Jesus' body, pretending that he did so to keep the body from decaying until after the feast.

These spices and herbs had great healing powers, and were used by our Esseer Brethren who knew the rules of medical science for the restoration to consciousness of those in a state of death-like fainting.' (The Crucifixion, by an eye-witness)

*'**Pretending that he did so**'*. What are we to make of this?

And *'**for the restoration to consciousness of those in a state of death-like fainting**'*.

We will consider both of these in a later chapter, when we look at Jesus taken from the cross.

But for now, let us return to those spices! What do we know about those same spices Nicodemus had been collecting to use on Jesus? We know they included myrrh and aloe.

In the Book of Exodus, in the Old Testament:

"The Lord said to Moses, 'Take the finest spices - 6 kilogrammes of liquid myrrh..........and make a sacred anointing oil, mixed like perfume......it must not be poured on ordinary men, and you must not use the same formula to make any mixture like it. It is holy and you must treat it as holy'. " (Exodus 30:22-33)

The New Testament refers to myrrh several times. Matthew tells us it was one of the three gifts, along with gold and frankincense, brought to the infant Jesus by the three Wise Kings. Then Mark tells us:

'There (Golgotha) they gave him wine mixed with a drug called myrrh, but Jesus would not drink.' (Mark 15:23)

Myrrh was used medicinally to reduce swelling and stop pain. Even today, it is used in Chinese medicine to improve the heart rate, blood pressure, breathing, and immune function.

Aloe has been identified as the oldest of medicinal plants, and has long been associated with healing. It is especially effective in the treatment of burns.

We now know too that Nicodemus used balsam:

'Nicodemus spread balsam in both the nail-pierced hands, but he believed that it was not best to close up the wound in Jesus' side, because he considered the flow of blood and water therefrom helpful to respiration and beneficial in the renewing of life.' (The Crucifixion by an eye-witness)

So myrrh, aloe and balsam were the main spices administered to Jesus by Nicodemus. Myrrh, aloe and balsam in a vast amount, that he had taken some time to gather up and procure. Myrrh, aloe and balsam that he knew he was going to need for Jesus.

But if Jesus was dead, surely myrrh, aloe and balsam would serve no purpose? Why would one apply such healing spices, and in such a large amount, to a dead body?

Furthermore:

'The body was then laid in the sepulchre which belonged to Joseph. They then smoked the grotto with aloe and other strengthening herbs, and while the body lay upon the bed of moss, still stiff and inanimate, they placed a large stone in front of the entrance, that the vapors might better fill the grotto.' (The Crucifixion, by an eye-witness)

Is there not an obvious conclusion to all of this?

Can we conclude that ***Jesus was not dead***?

Whatever went on in that tomb, it certainly was not a final interment!

And it could not have been an embalming! Embalming was an Egyptian custom, not a Jewish custom!

So to repeat, whatever went on in that tomb, ***it could not have been a burial!***

Eileen McCourt

CHAPTER 8:

The centurion and the spear wound

So far, we have seen what appears to have been a very detailed and ingenious plan instigated by Joseph of Arimathea and carried out by himself and his associates, in particular Nicodemus. The new tomb, conveniently placed near the crucifixion site in order to facilitate the speedy transfer of the '*body*' of Jesus to a place of safety and healing as quickly as possible. The timely creation of that tomb, just before the Crucifixion of Jesus, and disguised as being for Joseph of Arimathea himself, and therefore not arousing any unnecessary suspicion. Then we have Nicodemus and the enormous amount of healing herbs collected over a period of time.

And of course, let us not miss the fact that all four gospels emphasise the approaching Sabbath and how the body needed to be buried before that! The perfect smoke-screen! The Sabbath and the necessity for haste in getting the body off the cross and into the tomb for the supposed burial! No one would suspect anything! That perfect timing, surely, of the crucifixion itself! Taking place on the Day of Preparation, a Friday, which was the day before the Sabbath. And dead bodies had to be removed before the Sabbath. Certainly an advantage for Joseph and his ingenious plan! Haste was vital to the success of his plan, and to be seen to be hurrying in order to bury the body before the Sabbath was certainly a very credible smoke screen! No suspicions would have been aroused or questions asked surrounding that!

38

Now let us look further into this plan of Joseph of Arimathea! Apart from Joseph himself and Nicodemus, who else may have been in on it?

We need to take a look at the centurion and the spear wound he inflicted on Jesus! What do we know about that centurion?

Each and every image we see of Jesus on the cross shows a spear wound on his right side. And it is widely believed that Jesus did indeed suffer a spear wound. After the alleged 'resurrection' when Jesus appears to his disciples:

"A week later, the disciples were together again indoors, and Thomas was with them. The doors were locked, but Jesus came and stood among them and said, 'Peace be with you'. Then he said to Thomas, 'Put your finger here, and look at my hands; then stretch out your hand and put it in my side.' " (John 20:26-27)

So here we have Jesus pointing out the wound in his side. However, neither Mark, Matthew nor Luke mention such an incident. It is only in John that we read about the piercing of Jesus' side with a spear:

'Then the Jewish authorities asked Pilate to allow them to break the legs of the men who had been crucified, and to take the bodies down from the crosses. They requested this because it was Friday, and they did not want the bodies to stay on the crosses on the Sabbath, since the coming Sabbath was especially holy. So the soldiers went and broke the legs of the first man and then of the other man who had been crucified with Jesus. But when they came to Jesus, they saw that he was already dead, so they did not break his legs. One of the soldiers, however, plunged his spear into Jesus'

side, and at once blood and water poured out.'   (John 19:31-34)

A few points to consider here!

Firstly, there is no mention, in this one and only piece of writing describing this incident, that Jesus was pierced in his right side. So who decided it was his right side? Where did this come from?

Secondly, the spear wound could not have been given as the final death blow. If it was, then why was it not put through the heart? That wound was obviously meant to signify if the body would show any signs of convulsions or life. The wound was close above the hip, according to all the religious images we see of it, made at an inclined angle, only piercing the skin, and not any internal organs. If Jesus was already dead, the wound would not have spurted out blood and water, as a dead body will not bleed from an external wound, the blood already congealed. A corpse does not bleed! Fact!

Thirdly, the soldier who pierced Jesus must have had some doubt about him being already dead.

John adds onto the story:

'The one who saw this happen has spoken of it, so that you also may believe. What he said is true, and he knows that he speaks the truth.' (John 19:35)

To what exactly is our attention being drawn here? Was John trying to tell us something? That **Jesus was not dead?**

And:

"This was done to make the scripture come true: 'Not one of his bones will be broken.' And there is another scripture that says, 'People will look on him whom they pierced'." (John 19:36-37)

Here again we have that consistent sentence which runs through all the gospels, about everything happening in order to fulfil the scriptures and the prophecies. BUT! The soldiers were Roman soldiers! They would most definitely not have known the scriptures or the prophecies! So how could they possibly have been in any position to fulfil them?

There is certainly something very suspicious and deeply mysterious about all this behaviour! Why did the soldiers, hardened, brutal and merciless as they were, suddenly seem to have compassion on Jesus? They must have been extremely disciplined soldiers to not break Jesus' legs after they had broken the legs of the other two. But Roman soldiers were not known for either restraint or compassion!

Surely it is obvious that ***Jesus was not dead! And is it not possible that he was not actually meant to die?*** Just to make it ***appear*** as if he was dead? And could those soldiers have been in on it? At whose command? The command of their centurion?

So what about this centurion? Who was he?

Mark's Gospel tells us:

'Pilate was surprised to hear that Jesus was already dead. He called the army officer and asked him if Jesus had been dead a long time. After hearing the officer's report, Pilate told Joseph he could have the body.' (Mark 15: 45)

"The army officer who was standing there in front of the cross saw how Jesus had died. 'This man was really the Son of God!' he said." (Mark 15:39)

"When the army officer and the soldiers with him who were watching Jesus saw the earthquake and everything else that happened, they were terrified and said, 'He really was the Son of God!' " (Matthew 27:54)

" The army officer saw what had happened and he praised God, saying, 'Certainly he was a good man!' "(Luke 23:47)

None of these gospels mention that army officer by name. But in the suppressed ***Gospel of Nicodemus*** we are told who he is!

'Then Longinus, a certain soldier, / taking a spear, pierced his side, / and presently there came forth blood/ and water.' (Gospel of Nicodemus 7:8)

And Longinus is also mentioned by none other than Pontius Pilate himself, in a letter to Herod, where Pilate gives his account of the Crucifixion of Jesus:

'Now when Procla, my wife, heard that Jesus was risen, and had appeared in Galilee, she took with her Longinus the centurion and twelve soldiers, the same that had watched at the sepulchre, and went to greet the face of Christ, as if to a great spectacle and saw him with his disciples.' (Letter from Pilate to Herod)

"But when the centurion saw / that Jesus thus crying out gave up / the ghost, he glorified God and / said 'Of a truth this was a just man'. " (Gospel of Nicodemus 8:5)

'And as the Jews regarded all this as extremely supernatural, so the Roman Centurion believed now in the divinity and innocence of Christ, and comforted his mother.' (The Crucifixion by an eye-witness)

The *'extremely supernatural'* referred to here is the earthquake that shook the area:

'Although our brethren did not dare to tell the people, as it is a secret with us, nevertheless they well know the cause of this phenomenon of nature, and believed in their Brother without ascribing to him supernatural powers.' (The Crucifixion by an eye-witness)

The same source tells us:

"The Centurion, observing my anxiety, looked at me, and in the manner of a friend, I said to him: 'You have seen that this man that is crucified is an uncommon man. Do not maltreat him, for a rich man among the people is now with Pilate to offer him money for the corpse, that he may give it decent burial.'

My dear Brethren, I must here inform you that Pilate often did sell the bodies of the crucified to their friends, that they might thus bury them.

And the Centurion was friendly to me, inasmuch as he had conceived from the events that Jesus was an innocent man. And therefore, when the two thieves were beaten by the soldiers with heavy clubs and their bones broken, the Centurion went past the cross of Jesus, saying to the soldiers, 'Do not break his bones, for he is dead'. "

43

Historical records do indeed testify to there being a certain Longinus, a Roman soldier, who served in Judea under the command of the then Governor, Pontius Pilate. It was under the command of this same Longinus that the soldiers who were at Golgotha served when Jesus was crucified, and it was Longinus who has been identified as the one who pierced Jesus' side with his spear. He was obviously deeply moved, enough to exclaim 'This man really was the Son of God'.

After the Crucifixion and Jesus having been removed to the tomb, it was Longinus and his men who stood watch at that same tomb. It is documented too that the Jews bribed them to lie and say that the body had been stolen away by Jesus' disciples, but they refused the bribe. Longinus himself returned to his native land, Cappadocia, where he taught and preached about Jesus. According to Gregory of Nyssa, who was bishop of Nyssa from 372 to 376 and from 378 until his death, Longinus later became the bishop of Cappadocia and was persecuted by the Romans in their deadly campaign against the Christians, earning for himself the title of Saint Longinus. There is a painting of Saint Longinus by Bernini in Saint Peter's Basilica in Rome.

Christian legend has it that Longinus was a blind Roman centurion who thrust the spear into Christ's side at the crucifixion. Some of Jesus's blood fell upon his eyes and he was healed. Upon this miracle Longinus believed in Jesus. However, there is no reliable evidence for this part of the story.

So could it have just been possible that the centurion was also in on Jopseph's plans? A secret follower of Jesus! And he 'came out' at the Crucifixion?

If that were to be established as the truth, then that would certainly explain a lot of the mysteries surrounding the gospel stories and the so-called death of Jesus on the cross and his subsequent alleged resurrection!

But there is still another piece of the jig-saw to find! Another part of the plan!

Jesus had to be **seen to be dead**. How was that going to be further accomplished?

We need to look at that drink that was administered to him. Was it just some sort of cheap wine as the gospels tell us? Or was it something else?

CHAPTER 9:

The use of vinegar

It is generally believed that vinegar has always been mentioned as being the drink Jesus was given on the cross. But from where has this come? Certainly not from the canonical gospels!

So what do they tell us?

'One of them ran up with a sponge, soaked it in cheap wine, and put it on the end of a stick. Then they held it to Jesus' lips........With a loud cry Jesus died.' (Mark 15:35)

'There (Golgotha) they offered Jesus wine mixed with a bitter substance, but after tasting it, he would not drink it.' (Matthew 27:34)

Matthew also tells us:

'One of them ran up to him at once, took a sponge, soaked it in cheap wine, put it on the end of a stick, and tried to make him drink it...... Jesus again gave a loud cry and breathed his last.' (Matthew 27:48)

'The soldiers also mocked him: they came up to him and offered him cheap wine.' (Luke 23-36)

'A bowl was there, full of cheap wine, so a sponge was soaked in the wine, put on a stalk of hyssop, and lifted up to his lips. Jesus drank the wine and said, 'It is finished'. Then he bowed his head

and died." (John 19:28-30)

This surely suggests that whatever the drink was, it was taken to the site for a specific purpose. There was hardly a bowl of cheap wine just sitting conveniently in the area of the crucifixion!

So, according to all this, cheap wine seems to have been it, mixed with some bitter substance.

But! In the Gospel of Nicodemus one of the suppressed gospels, we read:

'The *soldiers who mocked him, / and taking vinegar and gall, offered / it to him to drink.'* (Gospel of Nicodemus 7:7)

So here indeed, we have the mention of vinegar. But in a suppressed gospel!

And in another suppressed gospel:

"One of them said, 'Give him bile with vinegar to drink.' Having mixed it, they gave it to him to drink." (Gospel of Peter 16)

Furthermore:

'Jesus was consumed with thirst. His lips were parched and dry, and the pain was burning in his limbs. A soldier put a sponge dipped in vinegar on a long cane of hyssop, and from this Jesus quenched his thirst.' (The Crucifixion, by an eye-witness)

But the remarkable thing is, as all the canonical gospels report, after Jesus drank the substance, whatever in fact it actually was, he immediately died!

And we are told:

'These spices and herbs had great healing powers, and were used by our Esseer Brethren who knew the rules of medical science for the restoration to consciousness of those in a state of death-like fainting.' (The Crucifixion, by an eye-witness)

So what does that mean? *'For the restoration to consciousness of those in a state of death-like fainting'*? Does this mean that **Jesus was not dead** but in a deep faint?

The Gospel of Peter tells us: *'But he kept silent, as if he felt no pain'.*

Certainly, there is much evidence that death-like fainting could be brought on by the use of particular drugs. In Shakespeare's **'Romeo and Juliet',** Romeo takes the herbal potion prepared for him by Friar Laurence, and then Juliet, believing Romeo to be really dead, puts an end to her life in order to join Romeo in death.

Furthermore, Yogis and Yoginis can attain a state of suspended or arrested breathing. And Jesus was certainly well learned in the practice of Yoga, having spent his *'missing years'* in other countries learning such techniques!

So what was in that drink that was given to Jesus? That drink that according to the gospels caused him to lose consciousness and go into a deep state of unconsciousness. A deep state of unconsciousness that made him **appear to be dead**?

We can only speculate!

All four canonical gospels tell us that Jesus died, crying out *'in a loud voice'*. But how could Jesus, in his then present state, actually have cried out in a loud voice? He was struggling to breathe! Asphyxiation was what ended the lives of those crucified. So crying out in any sort of voice, never mind in a loud voice, would have been highly unlikely! And if whatever was in that drink rendered him unconsciousness, then this makes his crying out loud even more unlikely.

And of course, when Jesus is reportedly dead, there is the earthquake. Just two of the canonical gospels tell us about this. Mark only says:

'The curtain hanging in the Temple was torn in two, from top to bottom.' (Mark 15:38)

Matthew goes into greater detail:

'Then the curtain hanging in the Temple was torn in two from top to bottom. The earth shook, the rocks split apart, the graves broke open, and many of God's people who had died were raised to life. They left the graves, and after Jesus rose from death, they went into the Holy City where many people saw them.' (Matthew 27:51-53)

But what is the other side of the story?

'Soon the mountain began to shake, the surrounding country and the city commenced to rock, and the thick walls of the temple gave way until the veil in the temple parted and fell from its place. Even the rocks burst asunder, and the hewn sepulchres in the rock were destroyed, as were many of the corpses kept therein.

And as the Jews regarded all this as extremely supernatural, so the Roman Centurion believed now in the divinity and innocence of Christ, and comforted his mother.

Although our brethren did not dare to tell the people, as it is a secret with us, nevertheless they well knew the cause of this phenomenon of nature, and believed in their Brother without ascribing to him supernatural powers.' (The Crucifixion, by an eye-witness)

It is time now to turn our attention to the Essenes and their role at the crucifixion.

CHAPTER 10:

The Essenes at the Crucifixion

In a previous book, '*Jesus Lost And Found*', I went into great detail in describing the Essenes, their way of life and their importance in the life of Jesus.

There is now no doubt that Jesus was in fact a member of the Nazoreans, the Nazoreans being a branch of the Essenes. We have ample evidence of all of this, all well documented. Yes, the Essenes certainly did exist! But they were known under different names. Indeed, as an ancient Jewish sect, the Essenes are not mentioned in any of the canonical gospels or in any of the other writings in the New Testament. They are not mentioned any more than Mary Magdalene is mentioned in her connection to Jesus. Maybe because they were so secretive and mysterious? Certainly every member of the Order was required to take a sacred oath at their initiation to never disclose any of the secrets of the Order to any person who did not belong to their community, and not to disclose to anyone else that he himself was a member.

But we have early historians and writers who do tell us about this secretive, mysterious Jewish sect. Obviously, those early Church fathers were not interested in Yeshua the man, only Jesus the god-man!

The first-century historian Flavius Josephus, together with Pliny, Dio Chrysostom and Hippolytus of Rome all spoke of this secretive and mysterious community of the Essenes. Dio Chrysostom, the Greek orator and philosopher also mentioned the Essene Community near the Dead Sea. His report is dated later than Pliny. While Josephus speaks of them as Essenes, mostly in Qumran, Philo of Alexandria speaks of them as the Theraputae, who are known to have been a branch of the Nazaraean Essenes. Many others refer to them as the Ebionites. Yet others simply as the Nazarenes. So the Nazarenes of the gospels are actually the Essenes. Jesus the Nazarene! Jesus the Essene!

"And so what the prophets said came true, 'He will be called a Nazarene' " (Matthew 4: 22-23)

BUT! This was NOT because he was from NAZARETH! Again, the gospels have misrepresented this information to us. Some scholars even claim that Nazareth as a place did not yet exist at the time of Jesus. If that is the case, and certainly Josephus does not mention Nazareth, then obviously the gospel writers have created a mythical Nazareth for Jesus their mythical god-man!

Publius Lentulus, when describing Jesus to Tiberius Caesar, the Roman Emperor, wrote that Jesus' hair was *'parted in the middle of his forehead, after the manner of the Nazarenes'.*

Hippolytus of Rome, writing two centuries later, gave a lengthy account of the Essenes, very similar to that of Josephus, but with some new material, though Hippolytus himself of course, was not an actual eye-witness to the Essenes.

These secretive, mysterious Essenes, who lived during the last two or three centuries B.C.E. and the first century C.E. were part of a vast extensive network system of Brotherhood extending through many centuries and many lands. They followed the teachings of ancient Persia, Egypt, India, Tibet, China and many other countries, transmitting all the knowledge in its most pure form. That esoteric knowledge was recorded in the Dead Sea Scrolls, found in caves in 1945 near the Dead Sea, where the Essene community of Qumran lived. In Palestine and Syria the members of the Brotherhood were called Essenes, with branches known as Nazoreans and Ebionites, and in Egypt as Therapeutae, or healers.

Their simple, pure, mainly agricultural, communal way of life, living on the shores of lakes and rivers, away from cities and towns, and sharing equally in everything, meant that there were no poor or rich amongst them. They established their own economic system, based entirely on the Law, and were living proof that all man's food and material needs can be attained without struggle, through knowledge of the Law. They were proficient in prophecy, healing, astronomy, all passed down from the Ancient Mystery Schools of Persia and Egypt. They sent out teachers and healers from their communities to teach the inner, esoteric knowledge to those outside the Brotherhood, to those who were ready to listen.

And two of those who were sent out from the Essene community at Qumran to teach and heal were John the Baptist and of course, Yeshua! Known as Jesus to us, known as Yeshua to the Essenes!

Even the Essenes themselves, secretive and all as they were, claimed Jesus as their own:

'In fine, Jesus was admitted into the Order at the same time with John in their years of early manhood. He lived then in Galilee and had just returned from a visit to Jerusalem, where he was watched

by our Brotherhood. Jutha was the place of his initiation, close by the grand castle of Masseda, where the mountains raise their lofty peaks above the surrounding country.

My dear Brethren, you may all have been convinced that he has been a member of our Order, as well by the doctrines he has taught the people, and his signs of recognition, especially the baptism and the breaking of bread and passing of the wine, as well as by his being baptized by one of our brethren, John, in Jordan, near the shore of the Dead Sea, in a westerly direction, - for baptism, as you know, has been, since time immemorial, a sacred institution in our Order. (The Crucifixion, by an eye-witness)

Not long after Acts of the Apostles and the canonical gospels were written, around 80 C. E., the Essenes were no longer in existence. Their teachings and doctrines had become heresy, their texts and writings being destroyed just like all the other texts and writings that did not agree with the teachings of the early Christian Church fathers. Those early Roman Church fathers who were not in the least interested in Yeshua the man, but in Jesus the god-man, created to compete with all the other Roman gods of the day, all born of virgins, all dying and resurrecting after three days.

But for the purposes of this book, we need to concentrate on the Essenes at the Crucifixion. We have already seen the important roles that Nicodemus and Joseph of Arimathea played, both of them Essenes.

Yes, it was the Essenes who took Jesus down from the cross.

'After this they hurried to the cross, and according to the prescriptions of the medical art, they slowly untied his hands, drew

the spikes out from his hands, and with great care laid him on the ground.' (The Crucifixion by an eye-witness)

But there is much more that has now been unearthed about the Essenes and their role at the Crucifixion!

'Therefore, my dear Brethren, we have kept these things a secret from the people, lest their belief in providence should be diminished. For you know there are many pious and excellent men who have recorded and remembered the life and death of Jesus, but have them only from rumours, augmented and corrupted by superstition; and from reverence and piety they believe what they hear of a beloved Master.

It was even so with those, chosen from among the people, who were called disciples of Jesus. Most of them have heard the story of his life and death only through tradition, as it has been told from man to man; although there were others who were present; but these have given no information concerning these important events.

In secrecy I will now inform you of what I and our Brotherhood in Jerusalem have seen and witnessed; and you know that an Esseer never permits aught to pass his lips save the strictest truth.

We might indeed have saved our beloved Brother from the vengeance of his enemies, if everything had not come to pass so quickly, and if our laws had not prohibited us from interfering in public matters.

Nevertheless, we have saved him in secret, as he fulfilled his divine mission in the sight of all the universe. Indeed, that a man die for his faith does not increase the glory of God; but that he, full of devotion and divine confidence, suffer himself to be subjected to martyrdom for his faith; and this resolution, firmly fixed in mind, constitutes the fulfilment of our work in the sight of the world.

Therefore, pay good heed to what I now tell you, that you may judge for yourselves of the rumours that have reached you hence from Rome.' (The Crucifixion, by an Eye-witness)

And:

'Dear Brother, you have reproached us, in that we did not save our Friend from the cross by secret means. But I need only to remind you that the sacred law of our Order prohibits us from proceeding publicly, and from interfering in matters of state. Moreover, two of our Brethren, influential and experienced, did use all their influence with Pilate and the Jewish council in behalf of Jesus, but their efforts were frustrated in that Jesus himself requested that he might suffer death for his faith, and thus fulfil the law; for, as you know, to die for truth and virtue is the greatest sacrifice a Brother can make.' (The Crucifixion by an eye-witness)

So here we clearly see another side, a secret side to the whole story of the Crucifixion!

Jesus himself was determined to have the prophecies be fulfilled. After all, that was what the Essenes had raised him for! That was their whole purpose in life! To raise Jesus to be the Messiah! And that entailed crucifixion for him.

The Essenes could not save Jesus from crucifixion at the hands of the Romans and Jewish authorities, because as they themselves said, their laws forbade them interfering in public matters or in matters of state. However, they could save him from actually dying on that cross. And make it appear as if he did actually die.

And saving Jesus from dying on that cross meant it all had to be carried out in the strictest secrecy. If the Jewish authorities were ever to find out that Jesus was indeed not dead, then they would go after him again and make sure they finished him for real this time. And not only Jesus, but also those who had helped him.

And it is not just in these ancient writings already mentioned, which all support and corroborate each other, that we get a different version of the Crucifixion. We have modern evidence as well! Very modern evidence in the form of new historical research! Synchronistic developments indeed!

Past-life regressions! Past-life regressions, where a person accesses memory recall into a former life! And what a valuable contribution to our research into the life and times of Jesus! Into the life of the Essene communities!

Dolores Cannon was a past-life regression therapist who, as part of her work, periodically met clients who had previously spent lives contemporary to Jesus. In her two best-selling books, *'Jesus and The Essenes',* published in 1992 and *'They Walked With Jesus'*, published in 1995, she gives an account of the recorded details delivered by clients who were part of the Essene community at the time of Jesus. These particular clients knew absolutely nothing about the Essenes prior to regression, and indeed after the session, remembered nothing. All the accounts support each other, even though these people did not know each other and had never met before in this life-time. What they delivered, under regression, supports the accounts of the early writers. More proof, indeed, if ever we needed more, of the existence of the Essenes and their importance in the life of Jesus!

And not just Dolores Cannon! We also have the combined work of Stuart Wilson and Joanna Prentis, who have spent the last twenty years researching the Essene communities, the life of Jesus and the powerful teachings of Mary Magdalene. They too have been using past-life regression to unearth amazing and fascinating evidence to bolster up our understanding of the ancient Essene sect, of whom Jesus is now without doubt believed to have been a member. Wilson and Prentis together published their best-selling 'The Essenes: Children of the Light' in 2005, followed by 'Power of the Magdalene' in 2009 and 'The Magdalene Version' in 2012.

Putting all this together, as well as the Dead Sea Scrolls, believed to be the writings of the Essene community themselves at Qumran, we now have a remarkable amount of reliable historical evidence and information, much more so than ever before.

These modern day regressions afford us access, bring us right into the Essene communities themselves! We are getting the inside picture! We are given the secret insights into this mysterious, secretive community, and indeed into their Core Group, the select inner circle who knew most about Jesus, and whose special responsibility was to protect Jesus.

Yes, Jesus was an Essene. As were Anna, the grandmother of Jesus, Joseph and Mary the parents of Jesus, Joseph of Arimathea the wealthy uncle of Jesus and the sister of Jesus' mother Mary, Mary

Magdalene and John the Baptist, all of whom together formed the nucleus of the surrounding support net-work set up to see Jesus fulfil his life-mission this time around. Coincidence? There is no such thing! Synchronicity? It all has to be! It can be nothing else!

The Essenes were a Jewish sect representing an esoteric, an inner, a spiritual aspect of Judaic Judaism. They were mystics, their totally pure way of life enabling them to access higher vibrational levels of spiritual energy far above the norm. They taught and practised astrology, prophecy, soul travel and psychic development.

And it was their skills in astrology and astronomy that enabled them to determine when and how the birth of Jesus would come about! They were the ones who interpreted the birth charts. They were the ones who facilitated the entire procedure.

The prophecies had said:

"The Lord says, 'The time is coming when I will choose as king a righteous descendant of David. That king will rule wisely and do what is right and just throughout the land. When he is king, the people of Judah will be safe, and the people of Israel will live in peace. He will be called 'The Lord Our Salvation'. " (Jeremiah 23: 5-6)

Of course, the Essenes knew the prophecies about the birth of the expected Messiah! They knew all the prophecies! And their main purpose, their main reason for being in existence, was to bring about the fulfilment of those prophecies.

Yes, it was the Essenes who arranged the marriage of Joseph and Mary, those two members of the Essene community who between them would meet the genealogical requirements specifically and essentially stipulated in the prophecies! This was to be a marriage which would produce the expected Messiah! And such a pair were of course, Joseph and Mary! Both Essenes! Both trained and learned in the Essene ways! And yes! It was the Essenes who determined all that! They knew the prophecies. They knew all about the promised Messiah. And their main purpose, their main function, their main reason for existence was to bring about the prophecy and see it through to the very end. The very end being, of course, the Crucifixion of Jesus. Hence their mysterious disappearance again shortly after the Crucifixion! They had fulfilled their mission!

The Crucifixion marked the end of their supporting Jesus, their Teacher of Righteousness. They had seen him through the task which was his destiny. The Crucifixion signalled the end of the whole development of the Essene communities, and it signalled the end of the highly spiritual Essene way of life.

Yes, the Essenes spawned, birthed, raised and fitted Jesus for his role as the Messiah for the Jewish people! They were the tailors who cut the cloth exactly according to the design! Jesus was tailor-made to order! Tailor-made in order to fulfil the ancient prophecies!

Lamb to the slaughter!

The Essenes protected Yeshua in his young life until he was old enough to be initiated into the secret Order as a member, with his cousin John. Yeshua, after becoming a member, knew all the secrets and duties of the Brotherhood. Yet he did not join one or other of their particular solitary communities. Jesus knew his mission was to travel and preach to the people, fully aware at the same time that he was putting his own life in danger. And when his life was in danger, the secretive Essene Brotherhood could not save him because their laws forbade them to interfere in public or political matters.

And another of the Essene teachings was that the highest reward, the greatest glory for any Essene was to die for the truth and faith! And Jesus had this firmly fixed in his mind as he travelled around the Galilee area, preaching and teaching the truth to the crowds and endangering his own life in the process. Jesus willingly suffered death in order that he might draw attention to the great truths of nature and its elements, rather than the superstitious beliefs instilled into the Jewish people.

At what particular and exact stage in his life Jesus learned of his destiny is of course, impossible to ascertain, but he certainly knew of it by the beginning of his ministry when he was 30 years of age, as he constantly referred to himself as the Messiah and fulfilling the prophecies!

And he certainly knew that those prophecies included his own Crucifixion!

So let us now return to the Crucifixion and what the Essenes were about at that Crucifixion! How did they fulfil their mission?

According to the past life regressionists Joanna Prentis and Stuart Wilson, the Essenes around Jesus at the Crucifixion were told not to look as Jesus was being taken from the cross, but to go about their business. ***ON NO ACCOUNT TO LOOK OR WATCH!***

'The core group absolutely forbade it. They were to continue with their lives, and make no further enquiries about Jesus.' ('The Essenes: Children of the Light', Stuart Wilson and Joanna Prentis, page 166)

Why were they given that stipulated command? What was it that they were not meant to see? Could it have been that **Jesus was not dead**?

Here again, we have that need for secrecy. Just as we saw with Nicodemus earlier on. Remember reading how Nicodemus:

'These (the spices) he wound about Jesus' body, pretending that he did so to keep the body from decaying until after the feast.' (The Crucifixion by an eye-witness)

Very clearly, the word *'pretending'* spells out secrecy!

As does:

'These spices and herbs had great healing powers, and were used by our Esseer Brethren who knew the rules of medical science for the restoration to consciousness of those in a state of death-like fainting.' (The Crucifixion, by an eye-witness)

What do the words *'for the restoration to consciousness of those in a state of death-like fainting'* mean?

What else can they mean except that **Jesus was not dead**, but only appeared to be dead?

The entire part played by the Essenes is riddled with secrecy and the need to maintain secrecy! And secrecy means cover-up!

Cover-up of what? Obviously cover-up of the fact that *Jesus did not die on the cross.*

And what about the alleged Resurrection? Was that cloaked in secrecy as well? Or did it ever even happen?

What has Josephus, the first century Jewish historian to say on that matter? Josephus tells us about the reports of the Resurrection. And he treats them as just reports, not facts:

"But for my part I know not which speak more correctly (those who say the body of Christ was stolen away or those who say that he rose from the dead). *But others said that it was not possible to steal him away, because they set watchmen around his tomb, 30 Romans and 1000 Jews."*

This large Jewish presence and the small Roman one are certainly not reported in the canonical gospels! Moreover, if this information from Josephus were to be true, then there is no possibility that Jesus' body could have been stolen away.

The suppressed Gospel of Nicodemus tells us:

"Then Nicodemus arose and / said, 'Ye say right, O sons of / Israel; ye have heard what those / three men have sworn by the Law / of God, who said, 'We have seen / Jesus speaking with his disciple / upon mount Olivet and we saw / him ascending up to heaven. / And the scripture teacheth / us that the blessed prophet Elijah /was taken up to heaven, and Elisha / being asked by the sons of the / prophets, 'Where is our father Elijah?'/ He said to them, that he is taken up to heaven." (Gospel of Nicodemus 11:1-2)

'And the counsel of Nicodemus / pleased all the people.' (Gospel of

Nicodemus 11:5)

'And when he had said these / things to his disciples, we saw him / ascending up to heaven.' (Gospel of Nicodemus 10:21)

This is the very same Nicodemus whom we have just seen *'pretended'* to wrap Jesus' body to prevent it from decaying until after the feast!

Now he is saying he saw Jesus ascend into heaven? Just like the prophet Elijah did?

What better way to throw the Jews off the trail of Jesus than to tell them he had ascended into heaven, just like the prophet Elijah had done? The Jews certainly believed in that! Sure was it not written in all their scriptures?

So, is it not apparent that there were two versions of the death and resurrection of Jesus put out there for Jesus' own safety? Only the inner core group of the Essenes knew the private version! It was the public version that was circulated for everyone else! And it is the public version that has been passed down to us through the Roman Christian Church.

But the private version clearly states that ***Jesus was not dead***.

CHAPTER 11:

Jesus taken from the cross

Cicero described crucifixion as '*the most horrible and frightening method of execution*'.

The aim of crucifixion was to extend the pain and misery of the guilty usually over a period of some days until they eventually expired. To prevent an easy or quick death, a small wooden cross-piece or suppedaneum was often fixed to the vertical post of the cross, on which the victim might prop himself up for as long as his strength allowed. Victims of crucifixion were left on the cross for days on end, as a warning and a deterrent, eventually eaten by scavenging birds, or, if they were taken down, the remains were thrown into a communal burial pit. Death, when it did come, was from asphyxiation after the legs of the victim were broken at the knee, rendering him unable to breathe.

It would be logical to assume that crucifixion always meant certain death. How could anyone endure that horrendous torture and yet remain alive? But, we have evidence from Josephus to the contrary:

"And when I was sent by Titus Caesar with Cerealins, and a thousand horsemen, to a certain village called Thecoa, in order to know whether it were a place fit for a camp, as I came back, I saw many captives crucified, and remembered three of them as my former acquaintance. I was very sorry at this in my mind, and went

with tears in my eyes to Titus, and told him of them; so he immediately commanded them to be taken down, and to have the greatest care taken of them, in order to their recovery; yet two of them died under the physician's hands, while the third recovered."

Indeed, if they were taken down from the cross after a relatively short period of time, a few hours perhaps, and before their legs were broken, then they could just perhaps survive.

The gospels all say that Jesus was nailed to the cross at the sixth hour (12 noon) and gave up his spirit at the ninth hour (3 p.m.) His rapid death was indeed, a matter of concern even to Pilate:

'Pilate was surprised to hear that Jesus was already dead. He called the army officer and asked him if Jesus had been dead a long time.' (Mark 15:44)

So not only was Jesus taken down from the cross after a relatively short period of time, just three hours, but, as we saw earlier, his legs were not broken. And as we also saw earlier, the centurion had specifically commanded his men not to break Jesus' legs.

And when they had taken him from the cross, what did they do?

'After this they hurried to the cross, and according to the prescriptions of the medical art, they slowly untied his hands, drew the spikes out from his hands, and with great care laid him on the ground.' (The Crucifixion by an eye-witness)

There is no mention here of Jesus' feet having been nailed to the cross. And none of the canonical gospels mention his feet being nailed to the cross either. And again, a week later:

"A week later, the disciples were together again indoors, and Thomas was with them. The doors were locked, but Jesus came and stood among them and said, 'Peace be with you'. Then he said to Thomas, 'Put your finger here, and look at my hands; then stretch out your hand and put it in my side.' " (John 20:26-27)

Jesus did not tell Thomas to look at his feet. Yet we have always been led to believe that Jesus was nailed to the cross by both his hands and his feet.

And let us not forget, the Essenes who were at the cross were told **not to look or watch**!

Was this because **Jesus was not dead**?

CHAPTER 12:

The rolled-away stone

All Jewish tombs had a large round stone rolled over in front of them at the entrance to the opening, often whitewashed, as we saw in an earlier chapter. That was all normal procedure.

But the rolled-away stone in front of the garden tomb of Jesus continues to puzzle us to this day.

First of all, we read in John:

'A week later, the disciples were together again indoors, and Thomas was with them. The doors were locked, but Jesus came and stood among them.' (John 20: 26)

So the doors were locked. Yet Jesus appeared among them. Obviously then, according to this, Jesus was able to move through locked doors. So if that was the case, then why was it necessary to have the stone moved away from the tomb? Could Jesus not just have gone through it without needing it to be moved?

Secondly, surely it would have been a better story if the stone had been left in place? Would that not have embellished even further an already elaborate tale? The disciples discovering that Jesus was gone, and the stone still in place? A supernatural happening? Adding more credence to the resurrection theory? Making Jesus into that supernatural being, that god-man, now fit for a particular purpose, that purpose of competing with other Roman and Greek gods of the time?

And of course, we are left wondering, who moved that stone?

In the Gospel of Peter, a suppressed text, we read:

'But during the night, before the Lord's day dawned, while the soldiers were keeping watch two by two......two shining men approached the tomb. But the stone which had been placed at the door rolled away by itself, making way in part, and the tomb was opened. Both the young men entered.' (Gospel of Peter: 35-37)

And shortly afterwards:

'Then the soldiers who had seen this woke up the centurion and the elders, because they were keeping guard too. And while they were explaining to them what they saw, they saw something else: Three men coming out of the tomb, with the two supporting one...' (Gospel of Peter: 38)

That one person who obviously needed support from the other two certainly does not seem to be someone who had just been resurrected from the dead!

"When they saw these things, those with the centurion hurried to Pilate by night, having left the tomb they were watching. They described everything they had seen....... Pilate responded, 'I am clean of the blood of the Son of God, and this is obvious to us.' Then all who came were begging him. They encouraged him to order the centurion and the soldiers to say nothing about what they had seen, 'It's better for us,' they said, 'to be guilty of a great sin before God than to fall into the hands of the Jewish people and be stoned.'

So Pilate ordered the centurion and the soldiers to say nothing. " (Gospel of Peter 43-49)

Here again, we have the plots and the cover-ups!

"The Jews hearing this, were / afraid, and said among themselves, / 'If by any means these things / should become public, then / everybody will believe in Jesus.' / Then they gathered a large / sum of money, and gave it to the / soldiers, saying, 'Do ye tell the people that the disciples of Jesus came in the night when ye were / asleep and stole away the body of / Jesus; and if Pilate the governor / should hear of this, we will satisfy / him and secure you.' / The soldiers accordingly took / the money, and said as they were / instructed by the Jews; and their / report was spread abroad among / all the people." (Gospel of Nicodemus 10:15-17)

" And having gone, they found the tomb had been opened. And having approached, they bent down and saw there was a certain young man sitting in the middle of the tomb. He was beautiful, having clothed himself with a long, shining robe. He said to them, 'Why did you come? Whom do you seek? Not that one who was crucified? He arose and went away. But if you don't believe, bend down and see where he was lying, that he's not there, because he arose and went to where he came from'. Then the women were afraid, and fled." (Gospel of Peter 55-57)

So here we have the crux of the situation!

The suppressed gospels simply say Jesus arose or got up or went away or is risen. They do not say that Jesus arose **FROM THE DEAD**!

The three synoptic gospels are the only writings that say Jesus was **raised from the dead.** But they are only **one** source, as we saw earlier, and not three independent sources as has been claimed!

"He is not here - he has been raised!" (Mark 16:6)

'After Jesus rose from death early on Sunday....' (Mark 16:9)

"He has been raised from death, and now he is going to Galilee ahead of you.' (Matthew 28:7)

"Why are you looking among the dead for one who is alive? He is not here; he has been raised. Remember what he said to you while he was in Galilee: 'The Son of Man must be handed over to sinners, be crucified and three days later rise to life.' " (Luke 24:5-7)

And we need to note here Luke's words: *'Why are you looking among the dead for one who is alive?'*

Is this saying that Jesus was alive, that he was **not dead**?

And those men in white? Who could they have been?

'Mary stood crying outside the tomb. While she was still crying, she bent over and looked in the tomb and saw two angels there dressed in white, one at the head and the other at the feet.' (John 20:11)

'One of our brethren went to the grave, in obedience to the order of the Brotherhood, dressed in the white robe of the fourth degree. He went by way of a secret path which ran through the mountain to the grave, and which was known only to the Order.

When the timid servants of the high-priest saw the white-robed

71

Brother on the mountain slowly approaching, and partially obscured by the morning mist, they were seized with a great fear, and they thought that an angel was descending from the mountain.

When this Brother arrived at the grave which he was to guard, he rested on the stone which he had pulled from the entrance according to his orders; whereupon the soldiers fled and spread the report that an angel had driven them away.' (The Crucifixion, by an eye-witness)

"And the brethren spoke to them as they had been ordered by those of the first degree, and one of them said to the women: 'Jesus is risen. Do not look for him here. Say to his disciples that they will find him in Galilee.' And the other told them to gather the disciples and conduct them to Galilee.

This was devised by the wisdom of Joseph, for he would not that they should look for Jesus at Jerusalem, for his safety's sake.' " (The Crucifixion, by an eye-witness)

Is this telling us that ***Jesus was not dead***?

CHAPTER 13:

'They have taken my Lord away'

In my previous book on Mary Magdalene, '**Behind Every Great Man: Mary Magdalene Twin Flame of Jesus'**, I explained in depth the important role Mary Magdalene played in Jesus' life. She was his '**Tower'**, his support, his spiritual equal, his partner, healing, exorcising and teaching alongside him throughout his ministry. A high priestess trained in the Temple of Isis in Egypt, she was the one who explained Jesus' teachings to the other disciples.

In the gospels found at Nag Hammadi, we see a very different Mary Magdalene from the Mary Magdalene of the canonical gospels. In these suppressed writings, Mary Magdalene is the target of the anger and resentment of many of the male disciples, Peter in particular, who constantly questions Jesus as to why he is telling her things he does not tell them, and why he loves her more than he loves them. Here, in these writings, Mary Magdalene is centre stage, the star of the show! But in the canonical gospels, she is conspicuous by her absence, only appearing at the end, at the Crucifixion. Bearing in mind the misogyny of the early Church fathers, it is almost as if they were forced to make a token acknowledgement of this powerful woman around Jesus, because to ignore her completely would greatly have reduced their credibility.

Mary Magdalene was one of the inner core group of Essenes around Jesus. A healer, she was there in the tomb, administering the herbs and spices alongside both Joseph of Arimathea and Nicodemus.

Yet in the Gospel of John we read:

'They have taken my Lord away and I do not know where they have put him!' (John 20:13)

These are supposed to be the words of Mary Magdalene. The words of Mary Magdalene as related only in the Gospel of John. Do these words suggest a robbery? Do these words suggest a resurrection from the tomb? Hardly!

And who were '***they***' supposed to be? Mary Magdalene obviously knew who '***they***' were! And those to whom she was speaking obviously knew as well who '***they***' were. The canonical gospels tell us that she was watching at a distance as Jesus was laid in the tomb. Standing watching. And then the gospels have her returning early on the Sunday morning to find the stone rolled away and the body of Jesus gone.

But other sources tell us she was in that tomb administering the medicinal spices. So how could she possibly have not known where Jesus was? Of course she knew that he was already in a safe hiding place!

Mary Magdalene knew that ***Jesus was not dead***!

CHAPTER 14:

The discarded dressings

'He saw the linen wrappings lying there, and the cloth which had been around Jesus' head. It was not lying with the linen wrappings but was rolled up by itself.' (John 20: 6)

Is there any significance in the head cloth being *'rolled up by itself'*?

'But Peter got up and ran to the tomb; he bent down and saw the linen wrappings but nothing else. Then he went back home amazed at what he had seen.' (Luke 24:12)

This is the first we have heard of any dressings! We certainly did not hear tell of any when Jesus was hurriedly taken from the cross and placed in the tomb! Then we were only told that they took his body from the cross and:

'Wrapped it in a linen sheet' (Luke 24:53)

'Joseph brought a linen sheet, wrapped Jesus' body in the sheet, and placed it in a tomb which had been dug out of solid rock. Then he rolled a large stone across the entrance to the tomb.' (Mark 15:46)

So from where have these dressings suddenly appeared? It's almost as if Jesus had been given a customary Jewish burial! But we have clearly seen that was not the case!

When Jesus first *'appeared'* to his disciples he was fully clothed.

Where did he get these fresh clothes? The last we heard of his clothes was that the soldiers had divided his clothes amongst themselves, as was customary at crucifixions.

So is it not obvious that Jesus was being looked after by someone? His Essene brothers?

And what about the rumours that his body had crumbled into dust? Surely a terrific smoke screen to prevent anyone looking for him? The Jews would certainly believe in such a story, deeply embedded in superstitious beliefs as they were!

'The news that the tomb was empty spread rapidly..........this vanishing into dust was a rumour which the core group had spread in order to protect Jesus. To say that his body had crumbled into dust, helped by the angels, was a most useful story. It explained why the tomb was empty, and also discouraged anyone from looking for the body. The core group did not want anyone looking for Jesus, alive or dead, and his security had to be considered.' ('The Essenes: Children of the Light', Joanna Prentis and Stuart Wilson page 175)

Indeed, if the '*wrappings*' had not been left, or specifically and intentionally placed in the tomb, then it would have been obvious that the body had been removed, dressings and all. But the fact that the dressings alone were there, furthers the Essene secret plot, surely?

All indicating that *Jesus was not dead*?

CHAPTER 15:

Pontius Pilate

Pontius Pilate was the fifth prefect of the Roman occupied province of Judea, serving under the Emperor Tiberius, from 26 to 36 C.E. He is mostly remembered and known for his role in the trial and crucifixion of Jesus.

But what more do we actually know about him? Opinions and judgements are diverse and even contradictory. Outside of Christian literature, Pontius Pilate is seldom mentioned in history. There are in fact only two contemporary writers who mention him, these being Flavius Josephus the first century Jewish historian and Philo of Alexandria, also a Jew. Then in the early second century, Tacitus the Roman historian added some more information. Each of these historians, documenting as they were, events in their own time, do not appear to have had any motive for recording details about either Pilate or Jesus to support the prevailing Christian writings. Indeed, there is an absence of supporting material in their writings, despite the fact that the gospels have Jesus performing the most wonderful and amazing of miracles.

As I explained in previous books, Josephus was a highly respected and much-read Jewish historian, especially amongst the early Christians. A native of Galilee, he was governor of that province for a time, prior to the war of 70 C.E. which saw the final destruction of Jerusalem. Thereafter, Josephus changed his allegiance, ultimately allying himself with Rome and the Romans.

Josephus' two major works were *'History of the Jewish War'* written in the 70s C.E. and *'The Antiquities of the Jews'*, written in the 90s C.E. However, probably the most remembered writing of Josephus is the famous *'Testimonium Flavianum'*, found in *'Antiquities'*, which is believed by most scholars to be an interpolation by early Church fathers to substantiate and bolster up their claim that Jesus died on the cross and was resurrected from death three days later. Yes, the alleged words of Josephus here were certainly a gift to the theologians and to the Church apologists! For them, surely proof if ever proof was needed? Furthermore, to add to the interpolation theory, the language of Josephus when narrating these same events has been described by scholars as the language of a Christian and not that of a Jew. The main culprit, according to most scholars, appears to have been Eusebius, one of the early Church fathers.

And what does Josephus say about Pontius Pilate?

'Pilate, at the suggestion of the principal men amongst us, had condemned him to the cross'. (Antiquities of the Jews, Book XVIII)

This at least confirms for us that a man called Pontius Pilate did exist, and that he was persuaded by the leading Jewish authorities to condemn Jesus to death by crucifixion.

Philo of Alexandria, also writing in the first century, refers to Pilate as the prefect of Judea and a man of *'Inflexible, stubborn and cruel disposition.'*

Tacitus, the Roman historian writing in the early second century, when describing how, after the great fire of Rome in 64 C. E. the Emperor Nero tried to put the blame for it on the Christians:

'Christus, from whom the name had its origins, suffered the extreme penalty during the reign of Tiberius at the hands of one of our procurators, Pontius Pilate.' (Tacitus, The Annals XV)

So there is evidence, outside of Christian literature, that Pontius Pilate did indeed exist. And then in 1961, in Caesarea in Israel, an inscription carved in limestone, and unearthed by archaeologists, referred to Pontius Pilate as Prefect of Judea, and related him to the reign of Tiberius Caesar from 14 to 37 C.E. That discovery ended once and for all any doubt for scholars that Pilate did indeed exist, and assured him his place in the history books.

As governor of Judea, Pontius Pilate had supreme judicial authority over the entire region, his main responsibility being to maintain order and to keep the money flowing into the Roman coffers from the onerous system of taxation imposed by the Romans on the Jewish people. But he did not have the military might at his disposal or the necessary military back-up behind him that he required.

 So how do the four canonical gospels portray Pontius Pilate? And why?

First, Mark:

"Early in the morning the chief priests met hurriedly with the elders, the teachers of the Law and the whole Council, and made their plans. They put Jesus in chains, led him away, and handed him over to Pilate. Pilate questioned him, 'Are you the king of the Jews?'

Jesus answered, 'So you say'.

The chief priests were accusing Jesus of many things, so Pilate questioned him again, 'Aren't you going to answer? Listen to all their accusations.'

Again, Jesus refused to say a word, and Pilate was amazed." (Mark 15:1-5)

'He (Pilate) knew very well that the chief priests had handed Jesus over to him because they were jealous.

But the chief priests stirred up the crowd to ask, instead, for Pilate to set Barabbas free. Pilate spoke again to the crowd , 'What do you want me to do with the one you call the king of the Jews?'

"They shouted back, 'Crucify him!'

'But what crime has he committed?' Pilate asked.

They shouted all the louder, 'Crucify him!'

Pilate wanted to please the crowd, so he set Barabbas free for them. Then he had Jesus whipped and handed him over to be crucified." (Mark 15:10-15)

So Mark tells us that Pilate made several attempts to sway the crowd. That same crowd that were stirred up by the Jewish leaders.

Next, Matthew:

"When Pilate saw that it was no use to go on, but that a riot might break out, he took some water, washed his hands in front of the crowd, and said, 'I am not responsible for the death of this man! This is your doing!'

The whole crowd answered, 'Let the responsibility for his death fall on us and our children!'

Then Pilate set Barabbas free for them; and after he had Jesus whipped, he handed him over to be crucified." (Matthew 27:24-26)

This is the only one of the canonical gospels that tells us about Pilate washing his hands of the blood of Jesus.

Now Luke:

"The whole group rose up and took Jesus before Pilate, where they began to accuse him: 'We caught this man misleading our people, telling them not to pay taxes to the Emperor and claiming that he himself is the Messiah, a king'.

Pilate asked him, 'Are you the king of the Jews?'

'So you say,' answered Jesus.

Then Pilate said to the chief priests and the crowds, 'I find no reason to condemn this man.'

But they insisted even more strongly. 'With his teaching he is starting a riot among the people all through Judea. He began in Galilee and now has come here.'" (Luke 23:1-5)

Pilate sent Jesus to Herod, who sent him back again to Pilate:

'On that very day Herod and Pilate became friends; before this they had been enemies.' (Luke 23:12)

"Pilate called together the chief priests, the leaders, and the people, and said to them, 'You brought this man to me and said

that he was misleading the people. Now, I have examined him here in your presence, and I have not found him guilty of any of the crimes you accuse him of. Nor did Herod find him guilty, for he sent him back to us. There is nothing this man has done to deserve death. So I will have him whipped and let him go'. (Luke 23:13-16)

"Pilate wanted to set Jesus free, so he appealed to the crowd again. But they shouted back, 'Crucify him! Crucify him!'

Pilate said to them the third time, 'But what crime has he committed? I cannot find anything he has done to deserve death! I will have him whipped and set him free'.

But they kept on shouting at the top of their voices that Jesus should be crucified and finally their shouting succeeded. So Pilate passed the sentence on Jesus that they were asking for. He set free the man they wanted, the one who had been put in prison for riot and murder, and he handed Jesus over to them to do as they wished." (Luke 23:20-25)

Finally, John:

"So Pilate went outside to them and asked, 'What do you accuse this man of?'

Their answer was, 'We would not have brought him to you if he had not committed a crime.'

Pilate said to them, 'Then you yourselves take him and try him according to your own law.'

They replied, 'We are not allowed to put anyone to death.' (This happened in order to make the words of Jesus come true, the words he used when he indicated the kind of death he would die.)

Pilate went back into the palace and called Jesus. 'Are you the King of the Jews?' he asked him.

Jesus answered, 'Does this question come from you or have others told you about me?'

Pilate replied, 'Do you think I am a Jew? It was your own people and the chief priests who handed you over to me. What have you done?' " (John 18:29-35)

"Then Pilate went back outside to the people and said to them, 'I cannot find any reason to condemn him.' " (John 18:38)

"Pilate went out once more to the crowd, 'Look, I will bring him out here to you to let you see that I cannot find any reason to condemn him'." (John 19:4)

"When the chief priests and the temple guard saw Jesus, they shouted, 'Crucify him! Crucify him!'

Pilate said to them,' You take him, then, and crucify him. I find no reason to condemn him'.

The crowd answered back,' We have a law that says he ought to die, because he claimed to be the Son of God'.

When Pilate heard this he was even more afraid. He went back into the palace and asked Jesus, 'Where do you come from?'

But Jesus did not answer. Pilate said to him, 'You will not speak to me? Remember, I have the authority to set you free and also to have you crucified'.

Jesus answered, 'You have authority over me only because it was given to you by God. So the man who handed me over to you is guilty of a worse sin'.

When Pilate heard this, he tried to find a way to set Jesus free. But the crowd shouted back, 'If you set him free, that means that you are not the Emperor's friend! Anyone who claims to be a king is a rebel against the Emperor!'" ....Then Pilate handed Jesus over to them to be crucified." (John 19:6-16)

So from the canonical gospels we get the clear message that Pilate made several unsuccessful attempts to sway the crowd and save Jesus from them. Furthermore, all four specify that it was at the instigation of the Jewish authorities that Jesus was brought to trial. However, what seems to have finally forced Pilate's hand was the threat, as related in John, that the crowd would see him as a rebel against the Emperor if he did not condemn Jesus.

And this is how most of us have come to know Pontius Pilate! Pontius Pilate, the Roman governor, who gave into the demanding crowds and signed Jesus' death warrant. Pontius Pilate, the man who washed his hands in public, of the blood of Jesus. And despite being warned by his wife against condemning Jesus:

'While Pilate was sitting in the judgement hall, his wife sent him a message: 'Have nothing to do with that innocent man, because in a dream last night I suffered much on account of him'. " (Matthew 27:19)

So here we have Pontius Pilate giving into the crowd!

'I am pure from the blood of the Son of God'. (Gospel of Peter)

He then commands the soldiers not to tell anyone what they have seen, so that they would not fall *'into the hands of the people of the Jews and be stoned'.* (Gospel of Peter)

This image of Pilate does not tally with other accounts of him, where he is portrayed as brutal, and as Philo of Alexandria described him,' *inflexible, stubborn and cruel'.*

Here was the man who had ridden roughshod over the Jewish people and, as related by Josephus, had insensitively paraded his offensive Roman standards in front of them! But he had withdrawn on that occasion, recognising his blunder. But he did not back down in the face of the opposition from the Jews when he re-directed temple funds to the building of an aqueduct. Many were brutally killed in the riots that followed.

Now the tables were turned! Now he was at the mercy of the Jewish leaders, those very same Jewish leaders who hated Jesus and desperately wanted him dead. They knew well the power they wielded in this instance, and used Jesus as a pawn in their power struggle against Pilate.

So what happened at the trial of Jesus?

Probably Pilate, being the shrewd politician he was, the opportunist, well practised in politics and political strategy, well versed in philosophy and familiar with ethics, decided to sacrifice one man in order to avoid a riot, a riot which he had not the military power at his disposal to control.

And why do the gospels depict him as the man who *'**washed his hands'**** of the responsibility of the death of Jesus? The man who *'**gave in'** to the crowd roaring for Jesus' condemnation? Why do all four canonical gospels go to great length to exonerate Pilate from the responsibility for the Crucifixion of Jesus?

Those who wrote the gospels, we must remember, were writing for a Roman audience! And so obviously, they would have endeavoured to avoid showing Pontius Pilate in a bad light! And obviously endeavoured to put responsibility for the Crucifixion of Jesus on to the Jewish people themselves, in particular, the Jewish leaders.

Yet, surely, at the same time, Pontius Pilate had the ultimate say. The ultimate decision was his, and his alone. Of course the Jewish leaders were the main instigators. But the ultimate decision lay with Pilate. And he knew he was condemning an innocent man to death.

But what if there was another side to Pontius Pilate?

Many scholars believe that outside of Christian literature, Pontius Pilate really did want to save Jesus, and would most certainly have done so if he could. They even suggest that Pilate may well have been a secret follower of Jesus. And if that is ever proven to be the truth, then that would certainly explain a lot of the mystery surrounding his actions in the trial of Jesus.

So where do we find evidence of this? The suppressed Gospel of Nicodemus tells us:

"And when Pilate had heard all / these things, he was exceedingly / sorrowful.' (Gospel of Nicodemus 8:8)

In the records of the Jerusalem Sanhedrin, there is a report from Caiaphas, the High Priest to the Sanhedrin, concerning the execution of Jesus. In this report, Caiaphas explains clearly why, in his opinion, Jesus was condemned to death:

'Nor was it because he claimed to be King of the Jews, nor because he said he was the Son of God.......nor because he prophesied or ignored the holy temple. No, nor all of these combined. There is a cause, and a more weighty matter, back of all these things that controlled my action in the matter............ the responsibility that rests upon me according to the laws of our Nation.......Jesus the Nazarene is a false teacher; for all he teaches is that a man's being sorry for a crime makes restitution towards healing the man he had injured.....but if man has nothing to do but repent, the disease carries its own remedy with it. So a man can sin as often as he may wish to.............God said to Abraham that once every year we should roast a kid or lamb, and eat it with unleavened bread, and this should be the sign that we would trust in Him in all times of danger. Now Jesus teaches that common bread and wine are to be used instead thereof - a thing unheard of. And not only so, something that is altogether repugnant to God, and something that fosters drunkenness, and is well qualified to excite men's passions.......Jesus says that he and his Father are one, they are equal. If he is right, his Father is false. If they were one, then their teachings would be one, and if his teachings are true, then God must be wrong....... by tolerating the teachings of Jesus, we say to the Romans that all our former teachings are false; that the Hebrew God is not to be trusted; that He is weak, wanting in forethought; that He is vacillating and not to be trusted, much less to be honored and obeyed. This is impregnating the whole atmosphere with moral pollution. It does not only cut off, but blocks the way of all Jews from heaven; and not only this, it excludes our hope in the salvation of our forefathers, who have obeyed God in His ordinances, believed in His promises.....Jesus entirely ignores God's holy temple - the house God had built by our forefathers under His own supervision, where he promised to dwell with His children, to hear their prayers, and to be pleased with their sacrifices..... the Temple is the bond of the Jews. Here all men can come and be blessed. It is the earthly home of the souls of men - the place where men may hide from the storms of sin and persecution. This temple is where the foolish

may learn wisdom, the place where the hungry may be fed, the place where the naked may be clothed..... Jesus says the priests have made it a den of thieves, and sets up a sneer, and even scoffs at its sacred ordinances, and with a sort of selfish triumph says it shall be destroyed..... But what would be the condition of our people if this temple was removed? What would be the use of the priesthood if the temple was destroyed? How would the soul of man be purified? My argument is that if this temple of God is destroyed, or even forsaken by the Jews, we as a nation are utterly ruined........ God says by mouth of Moses 'The Lord your God is one God; there can be but one.......But if you forsake me, then desolation will come upon you....Thou shalt pay to the Lord thy God once a year a half-shekel of silver.........' ....Could I stand and see all the holy ordinances, which have been appointed by our God for securing salvation to Israel, perverted by an imposter?.........Hence you can see the responsible position that I as the high priest of God and of the Jewish Church occupied. According to our laws I was made responsible, and stood between my God and my people, to protect them in doctrine and government.............We submitted to taxation to the Romans and the Romans are to protect our holy religion from foreign foes, in order that the holy temple or any of its sacred ordinances should never be molested, nor the holy city, Jerusalem, be polluted by Roman idolatry. Now the insinuating plan adopted by Jesus was well qualified to deceive the common people. It had already led many to forsake the temple, and hold their ordinances in derision, as well as to neglect the teachings of the priest or to pay the tithes for their supplies. He had already inculcated into the Jewish mind his pernicious ways of being saved to that extent that the Jewish cause was almost lost. The people to whom he preached were an ignorant set and knew but very little about doctrine of any kind. They are a restless sort of men, who are always finding fault and wanting something new, and never associate with the more enlightened part of the community in order to learn. Another reason for his having many followers is, his doctrines are congenial to unsanctified flesh. They are so suited to human nature that they require no sacrifices; they need not go to the temple to worship God; they need not fast; they need pay no tithes to keep up the temple or the priesthood, but every man can be his own priest and worship God as he chooses. All this is so compatible with human nature that, although he has not been preaching over three years, he has more followers today than Abraham has, and they have become perfectly hostile toward the Jews that are faithful to their God; and, if it had not been for the Roman soldiers, on the day of his execution, we would have had one of the bloodiest insurrections ever known to the Jewish commonwealth. I am told there was never seen such a concourse of people assembled at Jerusalem at the cross. One of my guards informs me that there were several hundred thousand, and, although there were two others crucified at the same time, Jesus was the great centre of attraction......... the soldiers had to use their spears to keep them back........... I was only accomplishing God's holy purposes, which exonerates me from guilt...........

Jesus spent two years in Egypt under the instruction of Rabbi Joshua and learned the art of thaumaturgy to perfection, as has never been taught in any of the schools of necromancy among the heathen. If the healing miracles of Jesus are true, and they are acknowledged by his foes as well as his friends, he must have learned them from Horus and Serapis as practised by those heathen priests. He came back to Palestine as a physician..... Jesus in the capacity of an itinerant teacher and physician roused the people of Galilee to repentance of sin, to bring about a restoration of the kingdom of heaven......... the breach grew wider and wider until an insurrection must have been the result........... he so far cut himself loose from the Jews that he ate with unclean sinners, publicans and lepers, and permitted harlots to touch him, while his disciples went so far as to eat their meals without washing themselves.......he looked upon the whole of the Levitical institutions, temples, sacrifices, and priesthood included, as no longer necessary...... he taught the repentance of sin, the practice of benevolence and charity, the education of the young, and good-will toward mankind, as possessing much more moral worth than all the Levitical cleanness, or compliance with the whole moral law given to us by our God to govern us........... his great object was to come as near the Jewish theology as possible so as to destroy the Jews' entirely, and establish his own........he was full of nervous excitement, all of which went to inspire his hearers with enthusiasm......he took but little care of his health or person; cared not for his own relatives. He travelled mostly on foot in the company of his disciples and some suspicious women, and lived on the charity of his friends........ the reprimands of Jesus were so severe against the rich and highly educated that they turned against him, and brought all the power they had, both of their wealth and talent, so that I saw a bloody insurrection was brewing fast..... the whole of the Jewish theocracy was about to be blown away as a bubble on a breaker......   as the Jews became more and more divided and confused, the tyranny of the Romans increased.......up to this time the Roman governors had shown great kindness to the Jews.....But Tiberias has turned against us; Pilate has removed the army from Caesarea to Jerusalem. I say, no nation with any self-respect, or one that had any energy left, would or could stand it without a struggle.......... I had issued orders to Jesus to desist from preaching, unless he taught as the Jews taught. He sent me the impertinent word that his doctrine was not of this world, but had reference to the world to come; when he was all the time doing all he could to destroy the peace and harmony of this world..........hence it is my duty to examine all the sermons of all the preaching priests, and if anyone teach the people wrongly, I must pronounce sentence for his crime upon him. This I did upon Jesus, to save the Church from heresy, and to save the cause of the Jewish commonwealth from final ruin. But understand that I did not act rashly or illegally, as I am accused. I only passed sentence under the protest and order of the whole court belonging to the high priest, containing twelve members, or elders, and priests.............and as we have conceded the right to the Romans of executing our criminal laws, it became my painful duty to send him to Pontius Pilate..................... I expected Pilate to send Jesus back to me, so that I could send him to you for your approval........but it seems that Pilate thirsted for his blood. Like all guilty tyrants, he was afraid of his own shadow, and wished to destroy everything that threatened his power.'

So this is what Caiaphas says of Pilate! That he *'thirsted for Jesus' blood'* and *'like all guilty tyrants, he was afraid of his own shadow, and wished to destroy everything that threatened his power'.*

We know there was no love lost between Pilate and the Jewish authorities, especially the high priests. They considered him weak, and he had offended them greatly when he insensitively paraded Roman banners in front of them, lacking any degree of respect for Jewish feelings.

Bearing in mind that Caiaphas, the high priest wrote this report to the Jewish Sanhedrin, explaining why he had acted as he did in the condemning of Jesus, and acknowledging that there is therefore bound to be a lot of bias in his report, there is still sufficient here to allow us to see the reasons why Jesus was condemned to death. He had upset the whole established Jewish set-up of wealthy corrupt priesthood and political leaders who all wanted him dead because he was destroying their livelihoods and all that the Jewish religion stood for.

But what has Pilate himself got to say?

We do have Pilate's report to Caesar of the arrest, trial and Crucifixion of Jesus:

'From that moment I was convinced that the conquered had declared themselves the enemy of the conquerors; and I would warn the Romans to beware of the high priests of this country. They would betray their own

mother to gain office and a luxurious living. It seems to me, that of conquered cities, Jerusalem is the most difficult to govern. So turbulent are the people that I live in momentary dread of an insurrection. I have not soldiers sufficient to suppress it. I had only one centurion and a hundred men at my command. I requested a reinforcement from the prefect of Syria, who informed me that he had scarcely troops sufficient to defend his own province. An insatiate thirst for conquest to extend our empire beyond the means of defending it, I fear, will be the cause of the final overthrow of our whole government.

A young man, it was said, had appeared in Galilee preaching with a noble unction a new law in the name of the God that had sent him. At first I was apprehensive that his design was to stir up the people against the Romans, but my fears were soon dispelled. Jesus spoke rather as friend of the Romans than of the Jews......................never have I read in the works of the philosophers anything that can compare to the maxims of Jesus.....One of the rebellious Jews, so numerous in Jerusalem, having asked Jesus if it was lawful to give tribute to Caesar, he replied: 'Render unto Caesar the things that belong to Caesar, and unto God the things that are God's'. It was on account of the wisdom of his sayings that I granted so much liberty to the Nazarene.................this man was neither seditious nor rebellious......I extended to him my protection, unknown perhaps to himself. He was at liberty to act, to speak, to assemble and address the people, and to choose disciples, unrestrained by any praetorian mandate. Should it ever happen, may the gods avert the omen, that the religion of our forefathers will be supplanted by the religion of Jesus, it will be to this noble toleration that Rome shall owe her premature death, while I, miserable wretch, will have been the instrument of what the Jews call Providence, and we call destiny.

This unlimited freedom granted to Jesus provoked the Jews - not the poor, but the rich and powerful. It is true, Jesus was severe on the latter, and this was a political reason, in my opinion, for not restraining the liberty of the Nazarene. 'Scribes and Pharisees', he would say to them, 'you are a race of vipers; you resemble painted sepulchres; you appear well unto men, but you have death within you'. At other times he would sneer at the alms of the rich and proud, telling them that the mite of the poor was more precious in the sight of God. Complaints were daily made at the praetorium against the insolence of Jesus.............Being too weak to suppress an insurrection, I resolved upon adopting a measure that promised to restore the tranquillity of the city without subjecting the praetorium to humiliating concessions. I wrote to Jesus requesting an interview with him at the praetorium. He came. You know that in my veins flows the Spanish mixed with Roman blood - as incapable of fear as it is of weak emotion. When the Nazarene made his appearance, I was walking in my basilic, and my feet seemed fastened with an iron hand to the marble pavement, and I trembled in every limb as does a guilty culprit, though the Nazarene was as calm as innocence itself........for some time I contemplated with admiration and awe this extraordinary type of man - a type of man unknown to our numerous painters, who had given form and figure to all the gods and the heroes. There was nothing about him that was repelling in its character, yet I felt too awed and tremulous to approach him........ 'Jesus' I said, 'for the last three years I have granted you ample freedom of speech; nor do I regret it. Your words are those of a sage. I know not whether you have read Socrates or Plato, but this I know, there is in your discourses a majestic simplicity that elevates you far above those philosophers. The Emperor is informed of it, and I, his humble representative in this country, am glad of having allowed you that liberty of which you are so worthy. However, I must not conceal from you that your discourses have raised up against you powerful and inveterate enemies. Nor is this surprising. Socrates had his enemies, and he fell a victim to their hatred. Yours are doubly incensed - against you on account of your discourses being so severe upon their conduct; against me on account of the liberty I have afforded you. They even accuse me of being indirectly leagued with you for the purpose of depriving the Hebrews of the little civil power which Rome has left them. My request - I do not say my order is - that you be more circumspect and moderate in your discourses in the future, and more considerate of them, lest you arouse the pride of your enemies, and they raise against you the stupid populace, and compel me to employ the instruments of law.'.............'Your blood shall not be spilt', said I with deep emotion, 'you are more precious in my estimation on account of all your wisdom than all the turbulent and proud Pharisees who abuse the freedom granted them by the Romans......... Insolent wretches!..... I will protect you against them. My praetorium shall be an asylum, sacred both day and night.'

So here we have Pontius Pilate affording protection to Jesus and allowing him to teach freely. No wonder Pilate incurred the wrath of the Jewish leaders! He was affording protection and allowing Jesus to speak freely! Jesus, whose main target was the Jewish authorities!

'Herod asked me what was my opinion concerning the Nazarene. I replied that Jesus appeared to me to be one of those great philosophers that great nations sometimes produced; that his doctrines were by no means sacrilegious, and that the intentions of Rome were to leave him that freedom of speech which was justified by his actions. Herod smiled maliciously, and saluting me with ironical respect, departed.'

Pilate defending Jesus against Herod!

And of that fateful day, Pilate says:

'The city was overflowing with a tumultuous populace, clamboring for the death of the Nazarene. My emissaries informed me that the treasure of the temple had been employed in bribing the people. The danger was pressing. A Roman centurion had been insulted. I wrote to the Prefect of Syria for a hundred foot soldiers and as many cavalry. He declined. I saw myself alone with a handful of veterans in the midst of a rebellious city,

too weak to suppress an uprising, and having no choice left but to tolerate it. They had seized upon Jesus, and the seditious rabble, although they had nothing to fear from the praetorium, believing, as their leaders told them,. that I winked at their sedition,- continued vociferating: 'Crucify him! Crucify him!' Three powerful parties had combined together at that time against Jesus: First, the Herodians and the Sadducees, whose seditious conduct seemed to have proceeded from double motives: they hated the Nazarene and were impatient of the Roman yoke. They never forgave me for having entered the holy city with banners that bore the image of the Roman emperor; and although in this instance I had committed a fatal error, yet the sacrilege did not appear less heinous in their eyes. Another grievance also rankled in their bosoms. I had proposed to employ a part of the treasure of the temple in erecting edifices for public use. My proposal was scorned.'

And what does Pilate say about Herod?

'Jesus was dragged before the High Priest and condemned to death. It was then the High Priest, Caiaphas, performed a divisory act of submission. He sent his prisoner to me to confirm his condemnation and secure his execution. I answered him that, as Jesus was a Galilean, the affair came under Herod's jurisdiction , and ordered him to be sent thither. The wily tetrarch professed humility, and, protesting his deference to the lieutenant of Caesar, he committed the fate of the man to my hands. Soon my palace assumed the aspect of a besieged citadel. Every moment increased the number of the malcontents. Jerusalem was inundated with crowds from the mountains. All Judea seemed to be pouring into the city.'

Pilate tells us how he was warned by his wife:

'I had taken a wife from among the Gauls, who pretended to see into futurity. Weeping and throwing herself at my feet, she said to me: 'Beware, beware, and touch not this man; for he is holy. Last night I saw

him in a vision...........Ah! Pilate, evil awaits thee. If thou wilt not listen to the vows of thy wife, dread the curse of a Roman Senate; dread the frowns of Caesar.'

'By this time the marble stairs groaned under the weight of the multitude. The Nazarene was brought back to me. I proceeded to the halls of justice, followed by my guard, and asked the people in a severe tone what they demanded...........the vociferations of the infuriated mob shook the palace to its foundations.'

'There was but one who appeared to be calm in the midst of the vast multitude; it was the Nazarene. After many fruitless attempts to protect him from the fury of his merciless persecutors, I adopted a measure which at the moment appeared to me to be the only one that could save his life. I proposed, as it was their custom, to deliver a prisoner on such occasions, to release Jesus and let him go free, that he might be the scapegoat, as they called it; but they said Jesus must be crucified..............'

'I then spoke to them of the inconsistency of their course being incompatible with their laws, but they still cried, 'Crucify him! Crucify him!'..............I then ordered Jesus to be scourged, hoping this might satisfy them; but it only increased their fury. I then called for a basin, and washed my hands in the presence of the clamorous multitude, thus testifying that in my judgement Jesus of Nazareth had done nothing deserving of death; but in vain. It was his life these wretches thirsted for.'

'Often in our civil commotions have I witnessed the furious anger of the multitude, but nothing could be compared to what I witnessed on this occasion.........the crowd appeared not to walk, but to be borne off and whirled as a vortex, rolling along in living waves from the portals of the praetorium even unto Mount Zion, with howling screams, shrieks, and vociferations such as were never heard in the tumults of the forum.'

'I, the continued governor of a rebellious province, was leaning against a

column of my basilic, contemplating the dreary gloom these fiends dragging to execution the innocent Nazarene. All around me was deserted. An air of desolation and sadness enveloped me. My guards had joined the cavalry, and the centurion, with a display of power, was endeavouring to keep order. I was left alone and my breaking heart admonished me that what was passing at that moment appertained rather to the history of the gods than that of men........Near the first hour of the night I threw my mantle around me and went down into the city towards the gates of Golgotha. The sacrifice was consummated. The crowd was returning home, still agitated, it is true, but gloomy, taciturn, and desperate. What they had witnessed had stricken them with terror and remorse. I saw my little Roman cohort pass by mournfully, the standard-bearer having veiled his eagle in token of grief; and I overheard some of the Jewish soldiers murmuring strange words which I did not understand.......... I returned to the praetorium, sad and pensive. On ascending the stairs, the steps of which were still stained with the blood of the Nazarene, I perceived an old man in a suppliant posture. He threw himself at my feet and wept most bitterly. It is painful to see an old man weep, and my heart being already overcharged with grief, we, though strangers, wept together.............those who betrayed and sold him, those who testified against him, those who cried 'Crucify him, we have his blood,' all slunk off like cowardly curs, and washed their teeth with vinegar.'

So what are we to make of all this?

Mark tells us:

'Pilate was surprised to hear that Jesus was already dead. He called the army officer and asked him if Jesus had been dead a long time. After hearing the officer's report, Pilate told Joseph he could have the body.' (Mark 15:44)

We are indeed getting mixed messages with regards to Pontius Pilate!

Was he really the weak man as the gospels portray him, who gave in to the demands of the crowd? Was it really just as simple as that?

Or was he aware of his weak military state, and therefore could not risk a riot breaking out?

Or was Pilate playing a crafty political game? A clever move in his constant battles with the Jewish authorities and high priests?

Or was he a secret follower of Jesus? A follower who had played a part in the plan to keep Jesus alive? That would possibly explain why he was surprised to hear that Jesus was already dead. And why he himself, according to his own report, was so morose and down-hearted after the alleged death of Jesus.

And if indeed Pontius Pilate was a secret follower of Jesus, then that would certainly explain his behaviour at the trial of Jesus! But at the same time he had to sacrifice Jesus, one man, in order to maintain peace and avoid serious riots.

But just giving into the crowd is not the historical Pontius Pilate. There must have been a lot more to it than that!

CHAPTER 16:

Jesus after the 'resurrection'

We tend to forget the fact that no one actually *saw* the resurrection!

"Why are you looking among the dead for one who is alive?" (Luke 24:5)

We have already considered these words in Luke. Yes, Jesus kept telling them he was alive!

" But he said to them,' Why are you alarmed? Why are these doubts coming up in your minds? Look at my hands and my feet, and see that it is I myself. Feel me, and you will know, for a ghost doesn't have flesh and bones, as you can see I have'. " (Luke 24:38)

"A week later, the disciples were together again indoors, and Thomas was with them. The doors were locked, but Jesus came and stood among them and said, 'Peace be with you'. Then he said to Thomas, 'Put your finger here, and look at my hands; then stretch out your hand and put it in my side.' " (John 20:26-27)

He was certainly not a ghost!

'But Jesus spoke to them, comforted them, and proved to them that he was really flesh and bones. Thereupon they surrounded him, touched his hands.' (The Crucifixion by an eye-witness)

Furthermore, he asked for food!

'After he had rested Jesus still more fully proved to his friends that he lived as do other people, by asking for food. Inasmuch as the friends had already eaten, there was left some bread, honey and fish, of which he ate and was refreshed.' (The Crucifixion by an eye-witness)

'So he went in to stay with them. He sat down to eat with them.' (Luke 24:30)

"He asked them, 'Have you anything here to eat?' They gave him a piece of cooked fish which he took and ate in their presence." (Luke 24:42)

Jesus, when he was better able to get about after his wounds having been treated, wanted to continue his mission:

"After further consideration Jesus said: 'If my disciples are not convinced that I really live, and if I do not go forth among them, they will think me an apparition and a delusion of their imagination.

Joseph answered him and said: 'Let us advance John to the higher degrees of our Order, that he may be convinced of thy living, and may execute thy directions and inform the other disciples concerning thee'.

But the elders of the brethren were not willing that John should be admitted into all the secrets, inasmuch as he was yet only in the lowest degree, and they feared that in his ardor he might inform others that Jesus was here." (the Crucifixion by an eye-witness)

Here yet again we have that secrecy, and the dire need for it!

'You wonder that the belief in the supernatural and miracles should gain foothold in our midst, when you know that we all have to bear the responsibility for the actions of one of our members.

Therefore, you ought to know that the rumor is like a wind. When it commences it drives the pure air far ahead, but in its progress it receives all vapors and mist from the earth, and when it has traveled some distance it creates darkness instead of the clear pure air of which it was at first composed, and at last consists solely of the particles it has received during its progress.

It is even so with the rumors concerning Jesus and his fate.

Furthermore, remember that the inspired men, who have written and spoken of him, were often carried away by the spirit of enthusiasm, and in their devotion and simplicity they believed all the things told them about him by the multitudes who were even more simple-minded and superstitious than they.

Bear ever in mind also that, in accordance with our rules, the secrets of our holy Brotherhood at all times remained unknown to these writers, and that only our higher members had any knowledge about the secret assistance and protection Jesus received from us.

And finally, do not forget that our rigid laws prohibited us from interfering or taking any active part in the councils or plans of the rulers of the land.

Therefore we have acted quietly and secretly, and have suffered the law to run its course; at the same time we secretly aided and assisted our friend in ways which did not infringe the law and our rules.' (The Crucifixion, by an eye-witness)

The Jews were steeped in superstition, living in very troubled times as they were, and a strong God, strict, punishing and vengeful as he was, but with whom they were familiar, appealed to them much more than what Jesus was teaching, about the Kingdom of God being within. Any rumours would have spread like wild-fire amongst them, fuelling their superstitious nature. So the rumour of Jesus being raised from the dead, or the rumour of his body dissolving in the tomb, or whatever, would not have been difficult for them to digest.

And let us also remember Paul and what was reported to have happened to him on the way to Damascus! A miraculous event, by all accounts, but which Paul does not mention in his letters, as we shall see in the next chapter.

Such a miraculous happening, the event that allegedly changed not only his name from Saul to Paul, but changed his whole life! But to compensate for Paul not mentioning it in his letters, we hear about it no less than three times in Acts! And of course complete with contradictions!

"As Saul was coming near the city of Damascus, suddenly a bright light from the sky flashed round him. he fell to the ground and heard a voice saying to him, 'Saul, Saul! Why do you persecute me?'

'Who are you, Lord?' he said.

'I am Jesus, whom you persecute,' the voice said. 'But get up and go into the city where you will be told what you must do.'

The men who were travelling with Saul had stopped, not saying a word; they heard the voice but could not see anyone.

Saul got up from the ground and opened his eyes, but could not see a thing. So they took him by the hand and led him into Damascus. For three days he was not able to see, and during that time he did not eat or drink anything." (Acts 9:7-9)

In this account, Saul's sight was restored by Ananias, when at his touch, *"at once something like fish scales fell from Saul's eyes and he was able to see again."* (Acts 9:18)

But Paul himself gives an account of the same event twice, when he is on trial:

"Many times I had them punished in the synagogues and tried to make them deny their faith. I was so furious with them that I even went to foreign cities to persecute them.

It was for this purpose that I went to Damascus with authority from the chief priests. It was on the road at midday, Your Majesty, that I saw a light much brighter than the sun, coming from the sky and shining round me and the men travelling with me. All of us fell to the ground, and I heard a voice say to me in Hebrew, 'Saul, Saul! Why are you persecuting me? You are hurting yourself by hitting back, like an ox kicking against its owner's stick '

'Who are you, Lord?' I asked. And the Lord answered, 'I am Jesus, whom you persecute. But get up and stand on your feet. I have

appeared to you to appoint you as my servant. You are to tell others what you have seen of me today and what I will show you in the future. I will rescue you from the people of Israel and from the Gentiles to whom I will send you. You are to open their eyes and turn them from the darkness to the light and from the power of Satan to God.' " (Acts 26:11-18)

No mention of blindness here! And quite an embellishment from the first version! Luke seems to have got carried away in the telling!

"As I was travelling and coming near Damascus, about midday, a bright light from the sky flashed suddenly round me. I fell to the ground and heard a voice saying to me, ' Saul, Saul! Why do you persecute me?'

'Who are you, Lord?' I asked. 'I am Jesus of Nazareth, whom you persecute,' he said to me. The men with me saw the light, but did not hear the voice of the one who was speaking to me........I was blind because of the bright light, and so my companions took me by the hand and led me into Damascus." (Acts 22: 6-11)

But in the first account, we were told that the men with Paul heard the voice but could not see anyone. Now we are told that the men saw the light but heard nothing! Furthermore, in one of his accounts, Paul received full revelation on the spot, concerning what he was supposed to do. In the other account, however, he was told to go to Damascus, where he would be told what to do.

So, again, we just ask ourselves, did this event ever really happen?

Or could it have been the real Jesus whom Paul met on the road?

The real Jesus, who had **not been dead,** and was now living in Damascus with his Essene brothers for safety? Damascus, in the middle of Syria, was full of Jesus' followers. That was why Paul was travelling to Damascus in the first place, just two years after the alleged *'resurrection',* to flush them all out!

Let us now delve further into the character and person of Paul!

CHAPTER 17:

The source of the death and resurrection story:

Jesus or Paul?

Is it not a remarkable fact that nobody saw the Resurrection? Absolutely nobody! The very event on which the whole of Christianity is founded! And no one saw it! And it is not from Jesus that we get any information about it! So from where does our information about the Resurrection come?

Christianity is a relatively young religion, less than two thousand years old, compared to the older religions of Hinduism, Taoism, Buddhism or Judaism, all of which pre-dated Christianity by thousands of years. Christianity, as I have explained in a previous book, grew out of Judaism. Judaism is the parent religion; Christianity the off-spring.

The New Testament is the writings of the early Christian Church, all written after the supposed death of Jesus. Here we have the teachings of Jesus, information about his life, death and resurrection, as well as events in first century Christianity.

However, the order in which these writings have always been presented to us is not in fact, the order in which they were first written. We have always been led to believe that the four gospels of Matthew, Mark, Luke and John came first and in that particular order. These were followed by the Acts of the Apostles, then the

Epistles, a series of letters including letters from an author claiming to be Paul. This is the order and sequence in which they have always been presented to us.

But if we look at the dates in which they were written, we get a very different sequence! It is actually the Pauline letters that come first, written about 50-60 C.E. Then come the four canonical gospels, and in the order of Mark first, written in 70 C.E., then Matthew, written between 80 and 85 C.E., followed by Luke written 85-90 C.E.. These three together are known as the **'synoptic'** gospels, because of the close literary connection between them, Mark providing us with the first basic narrative, and Matthew and Luke simply repeating a lot of what Mark says. Finally, John's gospel, written between 90 and 100 C.E. presents a very different Jesus from the Jesus of the other three gospels, most probably because the apocalyptic end of the world which the first three gospels predicted did not actually come about, and so the story was changed!

So, as we have established, the Pauline letters come first, having been written almost thirty years after the alleged death and resurrection of Jesus. These are therefore the first **written evidence** we have, as everything before that was passed down orally. And as these were the first written, then the writers of the gospels would have had Paul's writings before them when they were writing.

These epistles, which make up the bulk of the New Testament, are letters written by the Apostle Paul to the churches he was instrumental in founding in various cities. What do we learn about the life of Jesus from these letters? Very little! And what do we learn about the character of Paul from these letters? A great deal! In fact, Paul's letters are semi-autobiographical, the most important person being Paul himself, the hero of his own writings!

But why, we must ask ourselves, has the order of these writings always been deliberately misrepresented to us? It was obviously something to do with the contents of Paul's writings! And obviously, it was something to do with what Paul wrote, that needed to be hidden until after the gospels were written! All the more remarkable when we consider the fact that the letters of Paul are wholly detached from any event in Jesus' life except for his Crucifixion and Resurrection and a brief reference to the Last Supper. And obviously too of course, it was necessary to disguise the fact that the writers of the gospels, writing after Paul, were influenced by Paul's writings!

So what then, do these letters contain? Why did Paul put such great significance on the death and resurrection of Jesus, and yet fail to mention any other aspects of the life of Jesus? Why is it just all about the death of Jesus for Paul? And about the resurrection? As we shall see, the gospel that Paul created and preached differed greatly from the gospel that Jesus and his disciples proclaimed to the Jews.

The Gospel of Jesus was known as 'The Way', and his followers 'Followers of The Way'. Jesus' teachings were in accordance with what the Old Testament predicted about a human Messiah reigning over a restored kingdom of Israel, and Israel only, a kingdom of peace and righteousness. The Jews believed the Messiah was sent for them, the Israelites, and them alone. To them, the Messiah was a human figure, not a divine being, but an earthly king, from the royal line of David, sent by God to lead them to freedom from Roman rule and oppression.

And, as will become clear, the Gospel of Paul was in stark contrast to the teachings of Jesus. Writing thirty years after the death of Jesus, Paul refers to "*my Gospel*", the gospel "*that I preach*" and the gospel "*which I teach in the churches everywhere*" (1 Corinthians 4:17), to differentiate it from what was being proclaimed by the remaining disciples of Jesus in the Jerusalem Church. In Paul's teachings, the human Jewish Messiah meant for the Jews only, became a divine saviour of all nations. For Paul, Jesus was a god, a deity, and a human sacrifice, dying on the cross to atone for the sins of mankind:

'As for us, we proclaim the crucified Christ, a message that is offensive to the Jews and nonsense to the Gentiles; but for those whom God has called, both Jews and Gentiles, this message is Christ, who is the power of God and the wisdom of God.' (1 Corinthians 1:23-24

These two diverse gospels caused great animosity between Paul and the original apostles, an animosity that, despite attempts in the Acts to disguise, is still very obvious.

In 70 C.E. Jerusalem was destroyed by the Romans. The destruction was so complete, that Josephus, the Jewish historian writing at that time, describes how it was impossible to now imagine that any people had ever lived there. The Jewish followers of Jesus, *'The followers of The Way'*, were scattered or persecuted. Now there was no opposition to the gospel of Paul. So Paul's self-created version was incorporated into the Gospel of Jesus, in many cases supplanting it. And why? Because Paul was writing for a Roman audience, a Roman Empire that saw Paul's teachings as being more attractive and more in line with their beliefs about other gods of the time. Roman authorities who acknowledged that, despite three hundred years of persecution, the Christians were still increasing in numbers! The Roman Emperor Constantine, who, in the early fourth century, decided to make this new Christian religion the religion of the Roman Empire, for political reasons, and political reasons only! To bring some sort of cohesion to the vast, straggling Roman Empire!

When Paul changed Jesus from the Jewish "*son of David*", sitting on David's throne, ruling a free Israel, restored to its former power and glory, to Paul's own idea of Jesus as a divine "*Son of God*", sitting on his heavenly throne, it became necessary to invent a god-like biography for him. Thus the manifestation of the virgin birth, the miracles, the resurrection, and all the other wondrous and amazing feats that the gospels have attributed to Jesus, all in competition with other Greek and Roman gods of the time! And it was this, Paul's version, that found its way into the foundations of the new religion of Christianity!

So who was this Paul?

First of all, he was the self-proclaimed thirteenth apostle. The thirteenth apostle who opposed the other twelve apostles! Paul, who never knew or never even met Jesus, about whom he professes to know so much! Paul, who only first appears on the scene thirty years after the alleged death of Jesus! Egotistical Paul, who claimed that he, and he only, had secret knowledge divulged and revealed to him through visions and visitations of the risen

Christ! Paul, who claimed that his:

'Call to be an apostle did not come from human beings or by human means, but from Jesus Christ and God the Father, who raised him from death.' (Galatians 1:1)

There it is! The reference to Christ being raised from the dead! And this was before the gospels were written! And it is **Paul and not Jesus** who says it!

Paul, who, in his own words, saw Jesus, not as a human figure, but a divine being, raised from death by God the Father. Paul, who was appointed *'apostle to the Gentiles'* during the split that erupted between Paul and the remaining apostles of Jesus after Jesus' death! And why was he appointed as such? Simply because he could get no recruits from amongst the followers of Jesus, and so had to look elsewhere, to those who had never heard Jesus preach and had never known the teachings of Judaism.

We know that Paul was originally known as Saul of Tarsus. In his first letter to the Corinthians, Paul himself tells us:

'I am a free man, nobody's slave; but I make myself everybody's slave in order to win as many people as possible. While working with the Jews, I live like a Jew in order to win them; and even though I myself am not subject to the Law of Moses, I live as though I were when working with those who are, in order to win them. In the same way, when working with Gentiles, I live like a Gentile, outside the Jewish Law, in order to win Gentiles. This does not mean that I don't obey God's law. Among the weak in faith I become weak like one of them, in order to win them. So I become all things to all people, that I may save some of them by whatever

means are possible.' (1 Corinthians 9:19-22)

A Machiavellian Paul! A Paul who ingratiates himself with whomever necessary in order to get what he wants!

Being born in Tarsus, Paul would have been well linked into the Hellenistic myths and religious cults. The term *'Hellenistic Religion'* is the term applied to any of the various beliefs and practices of the peoples who lived under the influence of ancient Greek culture and the Hellenistic period of the Roman Empire, extended by some scholars to 33 C.E. And the important thing to remember about Paul is that he was a product of this Hellenistic period, deeply embedded in the Roman and Greek myths associated with their deities and gods. Paul grew up on a diet of such religious cults and religions! And, ironically, Tarsus was the very place where the Roman cult of the God Mithras had its origins!

And how would the remaining disciples and followers of Jesus have viewed this new comer? How would they have viewed this new comer who was distorting and changing what they themselves knew from actually having accompanied Jesus on his ministry? And what would Jesus have thought about Paul? Paul who deified Jesus and made him into a god figure, something which Jesus never ever said he was or thought of himself as being!

Paul certainly and obviously has a sense of his own uniqueness and self- importance, displayed constantly throughout his letters. We see too, a very didactic Paul, a very narcissistic Paul, a very delusional Paul. And a neurotic Paul, who would indeed make an interesting case study for a modern day psychologist or psychiatrist! Add to this his boastfulness, his arrogance, his patronising and condescending, and he certainly would not top the poll in the personality or popularity charts!

Scholars mostly describe Paul as shortish and rather frail, unprepossessing in appearance or stature, and with an impulsive, impetuous and austere temperament and nature to match. His own feelings of inadequacy were no doubt compensated for by the zeal, enthusiasm and energy with which he pursued and persecuted the followers of Jesus. He suffered badly from blackouts and fits, which he blamed on demons:

'We wanted to return to you. I myself tried to go back more than once, but Satan would not let me.' (1 Thessalonians 2:18)

'But to keep me from being puffed up with pride because of the many wonderful things I saw, I was given a painful physical ailment, which acts as Satan's messenger to beat me and keep me from being proud.' (2 Corinthians 12:7)

Paul, who believes he is set upon by Satan or some other evil entity! A man who obviously has some sort of inner conflict going on!

'We know that the Law is spiritual; but I am unspiritual, sold as a slave to sin. I do not understand what I do; for I don't do what I would like to do, but instead I do what I hate. Since what I do is what I don't want to do, this shows that I agree that the Law is right. So I am not really the one who does this thing; rather it is the sin that lives in me - I know that good does not live in me - that is, in my human nature. For even though the desire to do good is in me, I am not able to do it. I don't do the good I want to do; instead I do the evil I don't want to do. If I do what I don't want to do, this means I am no longer the one who does it; instead it is the sin that lives in me.' (Romans 7:14-20)

What sort of reverse psychology is that? Obviously, a greatly disturbed Paul! Even a psychotic Paul! And what about his arrogance?

'Actually I would prefer that all of you were as I am...' (1 Corinthians 7:7)

'Imitate me then, just as I imitate Christ'. (1 Corinthians 11:1)

Jesus, whom he never even met!

'You must teach and preach these things. Whoever teaches a different doctrine and does not agree with the true words of our Lord Jesus Christ and with the teaching of our religion, is swollen with pride and knows nothing'. (1 Timothy 6:3-4)

'In the letter that I wrote to you, I told you not to associate with immoral people. Now I did not mean pagans who are immoral or greedy or are thieves or who worship idols. To avoid them you would have to get out of the world completely. What I meant was that you should not associate with a person who calls himself a believer but is immoral or greedy or worships idols or is a slanderer or a drunkard or a thief. Don't even sit down to eat with such a person.' (1 Corinthians 5:9-11)

Here we have a very judgemental Paul.

'Surely you know that the wicked will not possess God's Kingdom? Do not fool yourselves; people who are immoral or who worship false idols or are adulterers or homosexual perverts or who steal or are greedy or are drunkards or who slander others or are thieves - none of these will possess God's Kingdom. Some of you were like that. But you have been purified from sin...' (1 Corinthians 6:9-11)

And what has Paul got to say on women, marriage and celibacy?

'The man who marries does well, but the man who does not marry

does even better'. (1 Corinthians 7:38)

'A man does well not to marry'. (1 Corinthians 7:1)

'An unmarried man concerns himself with the Lord's work, because he is trying to please the Lord. But a married man concerns himself with worldly matters, because he wants to please his wife, and so he is pulled in two directions..... An unmarried woman or virgin concerns herself with the Lord's work, because she wants to be dedicated both in body and spirit; but a married woman concerns herself with worldly matters, because she wants to please her husband. I am saying this because I want to help you. I am not trying to put restriction on you. Instead, I want you to do what is right and proper, and to give yourselves completely to the Lord's service without any reservation.' (1 Corinthians 7:32-35)

'Now, to the unmarried and to the widows I say that it would be better for you to continue to live alone as I do. But if you cannot restrain your desires, go ahead and marry - it is better to marry than to burn with passion.' (1 Corinthians 7:7-9)

' I would rather spare you the everyday troubles that married people will have........ there is not much time left........and from now on married men should live as though they were not married..........for this world, as it is now, will not last much longer.' (1 Corinthians 7:28-31)

'A married woman is not free as long as her husband lives; but if her husband dies, then she is free to be married to any man she wishes, but only if he is a Christian. She will be happier, however, if she stays as she is. That is my opinion, and I think that I too have God's Spirit.' (1 Corinthians 7:39-40)

'The husband is supreme over his wife, and God is supreme over Christ. So a man who prays or proclaims God's message in public worship with his head covered disgraces Christ. And any woman who prays or proclaims God's message in public worship with nothing on her head disgraces her husband; there is no difference between her and a woman whose head has been shaved. If the woman does not cover her head, she might as well cut her hair. And since it is a shameful thing for a woman to shave her head or cut her hair, she should cover her head. A man has no need to cover his head, because he reflects the image and glory of man; for a man was not created from woman, but woman from man. Nor was man created for woman's sake, but woman was created for man's sake. On account of the angels, then, a woman should have a covering over her head to show that she is under her husband's authority'. (1 Corinthians 11:2-10)

'As in all the churches of God's people, the women should keep quiet in the meetings.......... If they want to find out about something, they should ask their husbands at home. It is a disgraceful thing for a woman to speak in church.' (1 Corinthians 14: 34-35)

'In every church service I want the men to pray, men who are dedicated to God and can lift up their hands in prayer without anger or argument. I also want the women to be modest and sensible about their clothes and to dress properly; not with fancy hair styles or with gold ornaments or pearls or expensive dresses, but with good deeds, as is proper for women who claim to be religious. Women should learn in silence and all humility. I do not allow them to teach or to have authority over men, they must keep quiet. For Adam was created first, and then Eve. And it was not

Adam who was deceived; it was the woman who was deceived and broke God's law.' (1 Timothy 2:8-15)

'Nature itself teaches you that long hair on a man is a disgrace, but on a woman it is a thing of beauty. Her long hair has been given her to serve as a covering'. (1 Corinthians 11:14-15)

Did Jesus not have long hair? The style worn by Jewish men, with a parting in the centre, locks flowing freely down each side?

Now let us consider Paul as an agent of the Romans! Their very own propaganda machine!

'Everyone must obey the state authorities, because no authority exists without God's permission and the existing authorities have been put there by God. Whoever opposes the existing authority opposes what God has ordered, and anyone who does so will bring judgement on himself. For rulers are not to be feared by those who do good, but by those who do evil. Would you like to be unafraid of those in authority? Then do what is good, and they will praise you, because they are God's servants working for your own good. But if you do evil, then be afraid of them, because their power to punish is real. They are God's servants and carry out God's punishment on those who do evil. For this reason you must obey the authorities - not just because of God's punishment, but also as a matter of conscience.

That is also why you pay taxes, because the authorities are working for God when they fulfil their duties. Pay, then, what you owe them; pay them your personal and property taxes, and show respect and honour for them all.' (Romans 13:1-7)

Taxation! The main source of unrest and hatred for the Jewish people! The burden of taxation imposed upon them by the Roman authorities was the main reason that sparked off most of the Jewish uprisings! And here is Paul telling them to pay their taxes! Paul, the Roman! Ingratiating himself with the Roman authorities!

No wonder the early Christian Roman Church adopted Paul's teachings! It suited them perfectly to do so! Free propaganda! Good old Paul! Paul who will keep order for us! And what has Paul got to say on slavery? Slavery! So prominent throughout the Roman Empire!

'Slaves, obey your human masters with fear and trembling, and do so with a sincere heart, as though you were serving Christ. Do this not only when they are watching you, because you want to gain their approval, but with all your heart do what God wants, as slaves of Christ. Do your work as slaves cheerfully, as though you served the Lord, and not merely human beings. Remember that the Lord will reward everyone, whether slave or free, for the good work they do.' (Ephesians 6:5-8)

'Those who are slaves must consider their masters worthy of all respect, so that no one will speak evil of the name of God and of our teaching. Slaves belonging to Christian masters must not despise them, for they are their brothers and sisters. Instead, they are to serve them even better, because those who benefit from their work are believers whom they love.' (1 Timothy 6:1-2)

Talk about brain-washing, propaganda and spin! Paul! The Roman propaganda machine! Even his teachings on vegetarianism must have been sweet music to Roman ears!

'Some people's faith allows them to eat anything, but the person who is weak in the faith eats only vegetables.......... You then, who eat only vegetables - why do you pass judgement on others? And you who eat anything - why do you despise other believers?...........My union with the Lord Jesus makes me certain that no food is of itself ritually unclean.......' (Romans 14:2-3; 10:14)

What else would early Christian Church leaders have welcomed from Paul?

'When people criticise me, this is how I defend myself: Haven't I the right to be given food and drink for my work? Haven't I the right to follow the example of the other apostles and the Lord's brothers and Peter and, by taking a Christian wife with me on my travels?.........We have sown spiritual seed among you. Is it too much if we reap material benefit from you? If others have the right to expect this from you, haven't we an even greater right?...... Surely you know that the men who work in the Temple get their food from the Temple and that those who offer the sacrifices on the altar get a share of the sacrifices. In the same way, the Lord has ordered that those who preach the gospel should get their living from it............ ' (1 Corinthians 9:3-14)

The Roman Christian Church adopted this! And here we also learn that Jesus not only had brothers, but that they were amongst his apostles, and they were married! And their wives accompanied them on their travels with Jesus!

'In the church God has put all in place: in the first place apostles. In the second place prophets, and in the third place teachers; then those who perform miracles, followed by those who are given the

power to heal or to help others or to direct them or to speak in strange tongues. They are not all apostles or prophets or teachers". (12: 28-29)

A hierarchy in the Church! Something, surely, which Jesus never advocated! But which the Roman Christian Church does!

We saw earlier how the early Church fathers changed the order of the writings in the New Testament to make it appear that Paul's writings came after the gospels, rather than before. That means that the gospels must have got their inspiration from Paul! Right?

So, let us look at some of the teachings of Paul that found their way into the gospels!

"I passed on to you what I received which is of the greatest importance: that Christ died for our sins, as written in the Scriptures; that he was buried and that he was raised to life three days later, as written in the Scriptures; that he appeared to Peter and then to all twelve apostles. Then he appeared to more than 500 of his followers at once, most of whom are still, alive, although some have died. Then he appeared to James, and afterwards to all the apostles.

Last of all he appeared also to me........" (1 Corinthians 15:3-8)

No mention of Mary Magdalene or any of the other women here! But the gospels clearly tell us that Mary Magdalene was the first one to see Jesus after the alleged resurrection!

'The Day of the Lord will come as a thief comes at night. When people say, 'Everything is quiet and safe', then suddenly destruction will hit them!' (1 Thessalonians 5:2-3)

'... when the Lord Jesus appears from heaven with his mighty

angels, with a flaming fire, to punish those who reject God and who do not obey the Good News about our Lord Jesus. They will suffer the punishment of eternal destruction, separated from the presence of the Lord and from his glorious might, when he comes on that day to receive glory from all who believe'.
(2 Thessalonians 1: 7-10)

Is it not obvious that the gospels were influenced by Paul? And that was what the early Church fathers were so desperately trying to hide! And what was it that Paul was teaching that brought about the rift between him and the remaining followers of Jesus? The chief cause of the rift between the remaining followers of Jesus after his death and Paul was the nature of Paul's teachings regarding the divinity of Jesus:

'God did not even keep back his own Son, but offered him for us all! He gave us his Son........Christ Jesus, who died, or rather, was raised to life and is at the right side of God, pleading with him for us!'
*(*Romans 8:32-34)

'Now that we have been put right with God through faith, we have peace with God through our Lord Jesus Christ.......it was while we were still sinners that Christ died for us! By his blood we are now put right with God........We were God's enemies, but he made us his friends through the death of his Son.' (Romans 5:1-10)

'If you confess that Jesus is Lord and believe that God raised him from death, you will be saved. For it is by our faith that we are put right with God'. (Romans 10:9)

'For the Gospel reveals how God puts people right with himself: it is through faith from beginning to end. As the scripture says, 'The

person who is put right with God through faith shall live'.' (Romans 1: 17)

'God made peace through his Son's blood on the cross and so brought back to himself all things, both on earth and in heaven.........but now by the physical death of his Son, God has made you his friends......It is this Gospel that I, Paul, became a servant - this Gospel which has been preached to everybody in the world'. (Colossians 1:20-23)

'If Christ has not been raised from death, then we have nothing to preach and you have nothing to believe.' (1 Corinthians 15:14)

'For I received from the Lord the teaching that I passed on to you: that the Lord Jesus, on the night he was betrayed, took a piece of bread, gave thanks to God, broke it, and said, 'This is my body, which is for you. Do this in memory of me.' In the same way, after the supper, he took the cup and said, ' This cup is God's new covenant, sealed with my blood. Whenever you drink it, do so in memory of me'. (1 Corinthians 11:23-25)

So it was these teachings of Paul concerning the divinity of Jesus and faith alone being the requisite for salvation that led to the rift between Paul and the remaining followers of Jesus. Paul tells us about this rift in Galatians, including the words he had with Peter:

'But those who seemed to be the leaders - I say this because it makes no difference to me what they were; God does not judge by outward appearances - those leaders, I say, made no new suggestions to me. On the contrary, they saw that God had given me the task of preaching the gospel to the Gentiles, just as he had given Peter the task of preaching the gospel to the Jews. For by God's power I was made an apostle to the Gentiles, just as Peter was made an apostle to the Jews. James, Peter, and John, who seemed to be the leaders, recognized that God had given me this special task; so they shook hands with Barnabas and me, as a sign that we were all partners. We agreed that Barnabas and I would

work with the Gentiles and they among the Jews.' (Galatians 2:6-9)

Then he continues:

'But when Peter came to Antioch, I opposed him in public, because he was clearly wrong. Before some men who had been sent by James arrived there, Peter had been eating with the Gentile brothers and sisters. But after these men arrived, he drew back and would not eat with the Gentiles, because he was afraid of those who were in favour of circumcising them. The other Jewish brothers and sisters also started acting like cowards along with Peter, and even Barnabas, was swept along by their cowardly action. When I saw that they were not walking a straight path in line with the truth of the gospel, I said to Peter in front of them all, ' You are a Jew, yet you have been living like a Gentile, not like a Jew. How then can you try to force Gentiles to live like Jews?' (Galatians 2: 11-14)

And all this tirade from a man who, we saw earlier, proclaimed to be all things to all people, being a Jew or a Gentile or whatever, according to the dictates of the moment!

Paul's self-righteousness combined, this time, with his arrogance!

Paul is promoting himself as the person who will bring the Gospel to the Gentiles; he will supply the means, the secret disclosed to only him, by God, which he will reveal to the Gentiles. So, having him to preach to them they will not lose out on the fact that Jesus did not get round to them when he was alive. They have Paul now!

Now, finally, let us take a look at the bigger picture!

Paul ended up in Rome, and we now have the Roman Christian Church, which bears a remarkable resemblance to Paul's church structure! Paul's teachings about being saved by faith alone is the corner stone of the Christian Church! Believe, believe, believe is their constant message! Don't question! Just believe! The ultimate word for the Church apologists! There is no argument against it!

At the Council of Nicaea in 325 C.E., this same Church chose to include no less than thirteen of Paul's letters into their biblical canon! And this at the same time as they left out other written gospels! After all, Paul's writings were not called the '*Pauline Doctrine*' for no reason! And it was the writings of this man Paul which were included in the teachings of early Christianity! Writings which excluded anything about the life or teachings of Jesus!

So, what are we to make of all of this?

Certainly it is blatantly clear that Paul's teachings differed drastically from the teachings of Jesus! The problem of his own sexuality gave him a strong dislike of sexuality and the sexual act, fuelling in him an ascetic doctrine of marriage that has dominated Church attitudes even until now. His dislike of the feminine, his misogyny, stands in sharp contrast to Jesus' companionship with women. Paul even denies Mary Magdalene her place in history as being the first person to see Jesus after the alleged resurrection.

Yes, Paul taught his own teachings! And that was the cause of the rift between him and Jesus' original disciples. Jesus' brother, James, was left in charge of the Jesus movement, and Paul split from him. Paul taught that the whole meaning of Jesus' life centered around the shedding of his blood as a sacrificial appeasement on behalf of mankind, and by that shedding of Jesus' blood, mankind was redeemed from sin. According to Paul, this doctrine of salvation, this doctrine that Paul himself concocted, this doctrine of the death and resurrection from the dead by Jesus, is the only means by which we can be saved. It is exclusively and solely the grace of God which brings us salvation. A person can be saved only through baptism, according to Paul, and can contribute nothing towards his own redemption. No good works, no change of lifestyle can help a person gain salvation. By claiming that one can further or gain redemption through such practices or works, Paul taught, is merely brushing aside or belittling the sacrifice that Jesus made for us in the shedding of his blood.

So, paramount and central to Paul's teachings is the death on the cross and the resurrection of Jesus from the dead, the belief in which and the acceptance of which is the only means by which we can be saved. And these teachings are NOT the teachings of Jesus! In fact, such teachings are totally alien to the teachings of Jesus! Paul does not incorporate even one single teaching or parable of Jesus in his epistles. What Paul does is advocate his own teachings and philosophies.

And those teachings and philosophies have become the Nicene Creed, the foundation stone of the Roman Christian Church! But they are not to be found in either the Lord's Prayer or the Beatitudes! The Lord's Prayer and the Beatitudes which are the teachings of Jesus!

And what about the word 'Christian'? Neither Jesus nor any of his disciples ever mentioned the word 'Christian'! According to Acts, the disciples were first called Christians in Antioch, under the tutelage of Barnabas and Paul!

"Then Barnabas went to Tarsus to look for Saul. When he found him, he took him to Antioch, and for a whole year, the two met

with the people of the church and taught a large group. It was at Antioch that the believers were first called Christians." (Acts 11:25-26)

So clearly, Christianity came from Paul's teachings, and not from the teachings of Jesus!

And we need only look at the words of the Nicene Creed to see that this is in fact the case! This same Nicene Creed on which the whole teachings of the Roman Christian Church are based!

'I believe in one God / the Father, the Almighty, / creator of heaven and earth, / of all that is seen and unseen. / I believe in one Lord, Jesus Christ, / the only Son of God, / eternally begotten of the Father. / Through him all things were made. / For us men and for our salvation / he came down from heaven: / by the power of the Holy Spirit / he became incarnate of the Virgin Mary, and was made man. / For our sake he was crucified under Pontius Pilate; / he suffered death and was buried. / On the third day he rose again / in accordance with the Scriptures; / he ascended into heaven / and is seated at the right hand of the Father. / He will come again in glory to judge the living and the dead, / and his kingdom will have no end. / We believe in the Holy Spirit, the Lord, the giver of Life, / who proceeds from the Father and the Son. / Together with the Father and the Son he is worshipped and glorified. / He has spoken through the Prophets. / We believe in one holy catholic and apostolic Church. / We acknowledge one baptism for the forgiveness of sins./ We look for the resurrection of the dead, / and the life of the world to come. Amen.'

Yes! The source of the story of the death of Jesus on the cross and the alleged subsequent resurrection is clearly to be found in **Paul's**

writings and teachings, and not in the teachings of Jesus!

And Paul's writings pre-dated the gospels!

So the writers of the four canonical gospels had Paul's writings before them when they wrote these gospels!

Eileen McCourt

CONCLUSION:

Resurrection or resuscitation?

What really happened in that tomb?

The chief writings we have that relate the death of Jesus on the cross and his subsequent resurrection are the four canonical gospels of Mark, Matthew, Luke and John.

Firstly, we have seen how these gospels were specifically identified and established as the foundation for the teachings of the Roman Christian Church, all other writings declared heresy and burned, and those who advocated them annihilated.

Secondly, we have also seen how Christianity and the Christian Church began, not with Jesus, but with the Romans, and was made the official religion of the Roman Empire under the Roman Emperor Constantine in the third century, as a matter of expediency, to bring some sort of cohesion to the vast, straggling Roman Empire. Jesus the man was transformed into Jesus the god-man in order to fulfil a mission, that mission of establishing a religion that would be acceptable to the majority of people within that Roman Empire. So Jesus was made into a supernatural god figure in order to compete with all the other Roman and Greek gods of the time, most of whom were born on 25th December and gained immortality through dying for mankind and resurrecting from the dead three days later.

Thirdly, we now know it was in the writings of Paul, Paul the

Roman, that the resurrection of Jesus was first aired. Paul the Roman, who never knew Jesus. Paul the Roman, whose writings became the foundation of the early Roman Christian Church. Paul the Roman who quarrelled with the disciples and followers of Jesus after the alleged death of Jesus, diverting the teachings of Jesus from love and compassion and finding the Kingdom of God within, right back to the pre-Jesus days of superstition and a vengeful God, the very things which Jesus tried to eradicate! Paul, who taught that Jesus died for our sins, and that faith alone is sufficient for salvation. Paul, whose writings, 'Acts of the Apostles' are all about Paul. They tell us nothing about Jesus. Only about Paul.

Fourthly, we have seen how these canonical gospels are unreliable and unsubstantiated as any sort of historical writings, littered with inconsistencies and contradictions, failing to pass any of the tests of reliability, authenticity or validity.

Fifthly, any other writings we have, such as those of the early century historians, the Dead Sea Scrolls, the findings at Nag Hammadi, other gospels, past-life regressions where those under regression could not possibly have known beforehand anything about what was to transpire in the session, or even indeed those Vatican documents which have been accessed and have made their way into the public domain, all tell us a very different story. Add to all these the writings and findings of modern researchers, recent television documentaries, recent film versions, and recent archaeological excavations, and we have a plethora of material which is at variance with the Roman Christian Church canonical gospels.

Sixthly, we have seen that the gospels are merely metaphorical, merely stories built around the fulfilling of the prophecies in the Old Testament, evidenced by the constant interspersion of such phrases as *'This was done in order to fulfil the scriptures ....* *This was said so that the prophecies might be* fulfilled'.

And furthermore, we now know a lot about the secretive Essene community, who are never mentioned in the gospels at all. That same Essene community who spawned, birthed and raised Jesus, known then as Yeshua, to be the Messiah, the one who would restore God's Kingdom on earth. The Essenes planned it all. And in great detail! From Jesus' conception right up to his Crucifixion and his alleged 'Resurrection'.

And as the Messiah, he was destined to die on the cross and resurrect again on the third day!

But it is in our study of those very same Essenes that we find the truth emerging. It is in our study of those very same Essenes that we unearth that well-thought-out plan! That plan to keep Jesus alive on that cross and resuscitate him in that tomb! That plan that changes our whole understanding of what really happened in that tomb. And that plan is evident too, if we read between the lines of the gospels, and in reading between the lines, we can see for ourselves that what they tell us happened could not possibly have happened at all.

Yes, Jesus was alive after the Crucifixion! And therefore he could not have been resurrected! Resurrection surely demands a pre-requisite! One must surely first need to be dead!

Joseph of Arimathea and Nicodemus, both members of the

secretive Essene community, and possibly assisted by the
centurion in charge of the Crucifixion, himself perhaps a secret
follower of Jesus, ensured that Jesus would survive the Crucifixion.
And Jesus could not be known to survive that Crucifixion, obviously
because if those same Jewish authorities who condemned him in
the first place should ever find out he was not indeed dead, would
come looking for him again to finish him off properly.

Yes, there were two versions put out about the Crucifixion and
subsequent death and Resurrection of Jesus!

The version for public consumption, and then the private version
known only to a handful of the Essene community, the inner core,
those who surrounded Jesus at all times. Not even Jesus' closest
disciples were informed about this private version. They could not
be trusted! Had most of them not fled in fear for their lives when
Jesus was arrested?

And at the helm of this elite inner core, directing operations, was
Joseph of Arimathea. The wealthy man of the gospels, the member
of the Sanhedrin and secret member of the Essenes.

Joseph of Arimathea, who planned well in advance the various
means necessary to keep Jesus alive. The conveniently placed new
tomb, near the place of Crucifixion, supposedly for Joseph himself,
but in reality to speed up the transference of Jesus to a place of
safety and healing ; Nicodemus with a large amount of healing
spices and herbs which had to have been gathered up over a
period of time; the short period of time that Jesus was on the
cross; Jesus' body buried in a linen sheet, yet in the gospels we are
told of the garments, including the face cover, all neatly folded up;

the rolled away stone; the drink administered to Jesus after which he immediately lapsed into a state of unconsciousness; the spear wound and Jesus' legs not broken. A very clever plan indeed! Add to all this the fact that Jesus' body was not washed or anointed, so as not to cause the wounds to open again. ***Jesus was obviously not dead!***

Yes, in this Great Awakening which is now going on all around us, our eyes are at last being opened to the truth! We can no longer deny the obvious! And the reason why the obvious has escaped us for so long is because we were never encouraged to read the gospels for ourselves. We were a captive audience, hearing only what was thundered out to us from the pulpit, all Church propaganda to keep us under control through instilling fear and guilt. A punishing, vengeful God who would punish us if we did not tow the line and bow down to the Roman Christian teachings and dogmas, accepting them as the teachings of Jesus. And of course, pay our money to those who had set themselves up as the only intermediaries between us and this remote God who demanded constant appeasement.

But the flood gates have opened wide, and can never again be closed! That dark period in history, that dark period where we were kept in chains by a powerful, controlling, mercenary, male-dominated and misogynistic so-called Christian Church, whose only aim was holding onto power and control. The wealthiest institution in the world! And that wealth that was so vast even in the Middle Ages, that Henry VIII closed down the monasteries! The Church had more wealth than he had! The Church had more power than he had! That same Church that Chaucer had previously exposed in his *'Canterbury Tales',* showing the corruption, the deceit, the money-making deviousness, the false, hypocritical and extravagant lives being led by those who were at the helm, those in the upper echelons, those at the very top of the pecking order of the hierarchy of power and control.

Yes, it is time for us to re-assess what we have always been led to believe as being the truth about Jesus dying on the cross for our sins, and his alleged Resurrection from the dead!

All that we read in the gospels surely points to the strong probability that what they tell us happened, never actually happened at all! *Jesus did not die on the cross, and therefore there was no resurrection.* But those Essenes who put out that fake news put it out to protect themselves and Jesus from any reprisal from the Jewish authorities. They could not possibly have foreseen that their story was to be used as the foundation for Christianity! They could not possibly have foreseen that the Jesus they tailored and brought up to be the promised Messiah would be made into a God-man by the early Roman Christian Church fathers for their own mercenary ends, a pawn in their power games.

And all the evidence we have from the numerous other sources, from both the early centuries and from modern research, show, likewise, that *Jesus did not die on the cross and therefore there was no resurrection*.

Fake news! It never happened!

Yes! Jesus survived the crucifixion, rescued and resuscitated by his Essene brothers in *that tomb,* to continue his mission, not in Jewish Palestine, where his life would be in extreme danger if he was ever found again. Next time, the Jewish authorities, against whom Jesus had fought so strongly, would make sure he was dead, and with his death, their livelihoods and positions of power would be maintained.

The public and the private versions! Like the two sides of the same coin!

The public version put out by the Essenes in order to safeguard Jesus' safety. The public version put out by the Essenes in order to make it appear that Jesus had indeed died and been resurrected, as the prophecies foretold. The public version that was picked up by the early Church fathers because it suited their purpose, and made into the Nicene Creed, on which the whole Christian faith is founded!

And the private version, the secret version, known only to a small handful of Jesus' closest followers, the core group of the Essenes. The private version, the secret version, that tells the true story. *The truth that Jesus did not die on the cross and there was, therefore, no resurrection!*

The story of the death of Jesus by crucifixion and his subsequent resurrection is, like all the other accounts in the gospels, metaphorical, and not to be taken literally as factual happenings.

It is the message that is important!

And what is the message that we are meant to take from the death and resurrection of Jesus as related in the gospels?

The message is that there is no such thing as death as we have been led to believe it to be. There is simply an ending to our physical body after it is of no further use to us. We simply discard it as we would an old worn coat and free our spirit to move onwards on our spiritual path. Like the caterpillar and the butterfly, we simply metamorphose into a different form of energy, onto a higher, lighter vibration energy level. Yes, we will survive death! We will transcend death! For we are not just a physical body! We are a spiritual body having a physical experience. Our spirit is eternal and immortal, destined to fly forever, uninhibited, into the vastness of eternity where there are no barriers, no curtailments, no absolutes and no finality.

Other Books by Eileen McCourt

Eileen has written thirteen other books, all of which are available on Amazon as either print copies or Kindle. For more information, visit her author page: www.eileenmccourt.co.uk

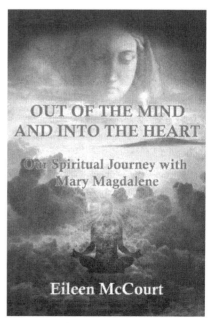

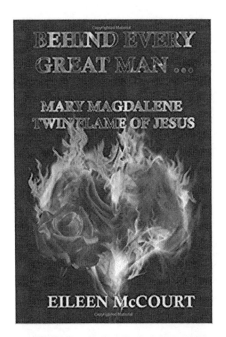

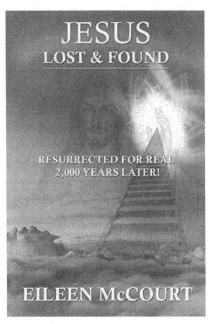

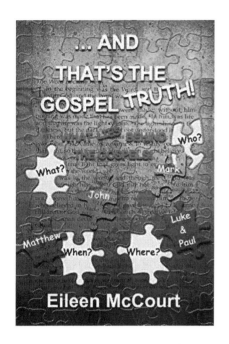

... AND THAT'S THE GOSPEL TRUTH!

WHAT IS BEHIND THE GOSPELS?

Who? What? Mark John Luke & Paul Matthew When? Where?

Eileen McCourt

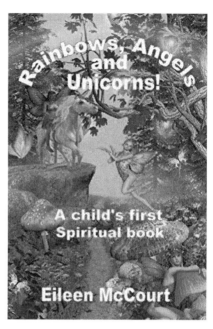

Rainbows, Angels and Unicorns!

A child's first Spiritual book

Eileen McCourt

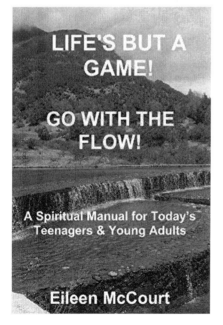

LIFE'S BUT A GAME!

GO WITH THE FLOW!

A Spiritual Manual for Today's Teenagers & Young Adults

Eileen McCourt

SPIRIT CALLING!

ARE YOU LISTENING?

Eileen McCourt

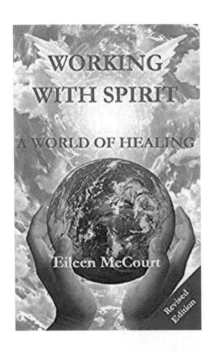

Printed in Poland
by Amazon Fulfillment
Poland Sp. z o.o., Wrocław